WEB OF
DECEIT

WEB OF
DECEIT

MISINFORMATION AND MANIPULATION IN THE AGE OF SOCIAL MEDIA

WITHDRAWN

Edited by
Anne P. Mintz

CyberAge Books

Information Today, Inc.
Medford, New Jersey

First printing, 2012

*Web of Deceit: Misinformation and Manipulation
in the Age of Social Media*

Library of Congress Cataloging-in-Publication Data

Web of deceit : misinformation and manipulation in the age of social media / edited by Anne P. Mintz.
    p. cm.
Includes index.
    ISBN-13: 978-0-910965-91-0
    ISBN-10: 0-910965-91-9
  1. Internet fraud. 2. Electronic information resource literacy. 3. Computer network resources--Evaluation. 4. Internet searching. I. Mintz, Anne P.
  HV6773.W423 2012
    364.16'3--dc23

                                                              2011033116

Printed and bound in the United States of America.

President and CEO: Thomas H. Hogan, Sr.
Editor-in-Chief and Publisher: John B. Bryans
VP Graphics and Production: M. Heide Dengler
Managing Editor: Amy M. Reeve
Editorial Assistant: Brandi Scardilli
Copyeditor: Barbara Brynko
Proofreader: Bonnie Freeman
Indexer: Beth Palmer
Book Designer: Kara Mia Jalkowski
Cover Designer: Dana Stevenson

www.infotoday.com

Contents

Acknowledgments

The authors of the chapters that follow deserve kudos for shining a light on the subjects of misinformation and manipulation in the age of social media. These contributors brought insight and creativity to the project, and I am honored that they agreed to take part. I thank them for their willingness to share their understanding about the pitfalls of using the internet as an information source along with their valuable advice on navigating around them.

In order of first appearance, the contributors to *Web of Deceit* are: Meg Smith, a crackerjack news researcher who reveals how social media can be used to deceive and defraud; Cynthia Hetherington, an expert in online intelligence and public records research who looks at identity theft and privacy issues; Eli Edwards, an attorney and researcher who shows how messages of hatred and intolerance are being spread in the digital age; Ben Fractenberg, a reporter and news producer who reviews a range of online criminal activities and the threats they pose to the unwary; Deborah A. Liptak, whose background in military communications and research informs her views on information warfare and the technologies of deception; Laura Gordon-Murnane, a webmaster and researcher who explores key intersections of news and politics, and how they impact our lives; Craig Thompson, a reporter and researcher who takes a timely look at how charity scams successfully target the philanthropic among us; and Amber Benham, a journalist and educator who presents a primer on the critical evaluation of information sources that is not to be missed.

John B. Bryans, editor-in-chief and publisher of the Book Publishing Division at Information Today, Inc., was immediately supportive of a sequel to *Web of Deception* (CyberAge Books, 2002). I was eager to work with him a second time. He trusted our collective judgment completely to make it happen as we envisioned it. John is a wise editor who made the text even better, and I thank him for his role in making the book come to life.

Amy Reeve, managing editor, contributed enormous professional expertise that is invisible to the reader but impacted every page of the book. The care she brought to the production process is truly appreciated.

Tom Hogan Sr., president of Information Today, Inc., is a good friend (still), who believes in me (still), and was willing to take yet another risk. He (still) disproves the cliché that one should never do business with friends.

To other friends and colleagues: Bill Barrett at Forbes, Joanna Hernandez at the *Washington Post*, cybersecurity expert Andy Norton, and the Anti-Defamation League's Jonathan Vick reviewed sections of the manuscript and provided excellent input. *Searcher* magazine's Barbara Quint helped to conceptualize the book and offered a number of useful suggestions. Their contributions are greatly appreciated. A big thank you to my professional colleagues, from whom I learn something new every day. And thanks to the rest of my friends for their unwavering support. It's been a great trip so far.

—Anne P. Mintz

INTRODUCTION

If It's on the Internet, It Must Be True

Anne P. Mintz

During the Winter Olympic Games in February 2010, actor Michael C. Hall narrated a television commercial:

> President's Day commemorates the day George Washington bought his first car. He was 16. And it was a Hemi V8 Dodge Charger. Then he met Martha and her kids and bought himself a seven-seater Dodge Caravan. And it was only when he moved back to Mount Vernon that he got an all-wheel drive V6 Journey.
> At least that's what it said on the internet.[1]

Even my 93-year-old mother laughed. She understands the unreliability of information found online.

The internet is a petri dish for the growth and spread of misinformation. While some incorrect information is either innocent or harmless, such as the clever ad for Dodge, that is not the focus of this book. Rather, I hope to shed light on the misinformation spread via the internet that is intentional, harmful, and manipulative in nature.

The Larger Context

Misinformation on the internet is dangerous and part of a much larger picture. Bending the truth or telling outright lies is not new. It's just the messenger who has changed, and this messenger spreads the word lightning fast and to far-flung places. In just the past decade, we have witnessed government leaders and chief executives of major corporations misinform the public in ways that have had enormous consequences, some involving life and death, and others contributing to financial ruin.

In 2002, the U.S. invaded Iraq based on reports that Saddam Hussein's government was stockpiling weapons of mass destruction, although scientists and inspectors tasked by the United Nations could not confirm their existence. The then-president of the U.S. addressed the American people and declared that he knew for a fact that these weapons existed. The contrary was later confirmed to be true. As of late 2011, U.S. troops are still in Iraq. Thousands of soldiers have lost their lives, and tens of thousands have suffered loss of limbs and psychological damage from serving in this war. The human cost extends to their families. The financial costs helped escalate a deep recession that began in 2008, costing millions of people their livelihoods and, in many cases, the roofs over their heads.

Enron, once a major utility based in Houston, routinely filed misleading federally required documents that investors and regulators failed to notice or investigate. In 2001, a reporter for *Fortune* magazine who thought some of the financial reports didn't add up questioned Enron executives. She wasn't satisfied with their answers. She kept digging, and the result was that Enron's then-chief executive and chief financial officers were convicted on 10 counts of fraud, conspiracy, and banking violations.[2] Their intentional misinformation resulted in thousands of Enron employees losing their jobs and shareholder investments being wiped out. The multinational accounting firm Arthur Andersen went belly-up, the result of its Houston office's failure to discover the fraud; the ripple effect touched thousands who worked at other companies doing business with Enron. Needless to say, the economic impact was deep and widespread.

In October 2010, pharmaceutical giant GlaxoSmithKline settled a federal lawsuit in which it acknowledged that it had knowingly manufactured and distributed ineffective pharmaceuticals to patients.[3] The company had intentionally misinformed patients about the efficacy of the diabetes drug Avandamet, the antidepressant Paxil, and the antibiotic Bactroban, among others, all of which had been manufactured at one plant from 2001 to 2005. An employee whose job had been eliminated blew the whistle on the pharmaceutical giant. It took more than 5 years for the company to accept legal responsibility and to agree to pay damages.

Even credit agencies that rate the viability of major corporations and other investment vehicles have come under fire for failing to check facts independently and failing to avoid conflicts of interest. Standard & Poor's, Fitch Ratings, and Moody's Investors Service were heavily implicated in the financial crisis that began in late 2008. Agencies that assessed risk in mortgage pools ignored what the *New York Times* described as conclusive evidence of dubious loans.[4] Failing to act on credible information at their disposal, the agencies awarded ratings that were woefully inaccurate. According to D. Keith Johnson's testimony given to the U.S. Financial Crisis Inquiry Commission in 2010, the agencies' reports calling mortgage pools "safe investments" intentionally misinformed the public. The ripple effects are still being felt by each U.S. taxpayer.

Connecting the Dots

There is a growing digital divide between people who are close to the facts and people who aren't. Historically, journalists and other information professionals have been the disseminators of the facts. It was their job to connect the dots and offer explanations. Even more critical, it was their job to tell us where the dots were and why they were important. Today, however, because of economic distress, major media organizations have cut back on investigative reporters, expert researchers, and fact-checkers. More than ever, we need help locating and connecting those dots, understanding when to believe authorities and sources, learning when to dig further to expose falsehoods, and determining where and how to locate accurate information. We must learn where to find quality information, how to evaluate the sources we encounter, and how to avoid being manipulated and victimized by online criminals.

In its 2011 annual State of the Net survey, *Consumer Reports* concluded that almost four in every five households use social networks, nearly twice as many as in 2009. It reported that one-third of the 2,089 respondent households had experienced some sort of online abuse such as malware infection, scams, identity theft, or harassment—more than double the percentage from 2010. *Consumer Reports* estimates that malware cost consumers $2.3 billion in the past year and caused them to replace 1.3 million PCs.[5] This is big business—not "much ado about nothing."

People using social media and the internet commonly make mistakes in judgment. Sometimes people unintentionally explore subversive websites, and sometimes people forget the potentially public and permanent nature of their online communications. Two members of the U.S. House of Representatives (Christopher Lee and Anthony Weiner, both of New York state) resigned in 2010 and 2011 after injudiciously sending photos of themselves using craigslist and Twitter. But that's not why we wrote this book. Our concern is that some unsuspecting internet users are not aware that they are engaging in risky behavior and that they are unknowingly encountering scams, downloading viruses, and purchasing stolen goods that help criminals launder money. How complicit are we in furthering the flood of intentional misinformation? And, more importantly, how can we counter it?

In this context, we will explore a number of key areas in which internet users often find intentional misinformation, in order to see the larger picture of how these lies and falsehoods are spread and how online criminal activity operates, so we don't become victims. The book is not intended to document every incident of intentional misinformation in these areas; the specific examples are not the problem but rather the symptom. We want to portray the larger picture of an international, unregulated canvas where these examples are the small dots. We also want to help you connect those dots and better understand the results of your internet searches.

Social Media and Unintended Consequences

In September 2010, police in Nashua, New Hampshire, arrested three men on burglary and related charges.[6] According to police, the property owners whose homes had been burglarized had posted their travel plans on Facebook. Police said they recovered from $100,000 to $200,000 worth of stolen property. By now, most Facebook users are aware of the dangers of posting such information, but there's much more to know.

Driven by younger, technologically savvy students, Myspace and Facebook have grown exponentially into sites where people can and do pretend to be who they aren't. Sexual predators and thieves who prey on the unsuspecting can pose as potential friends, with a goal of abusing or bilking the unwary. Given the broad coverage of the dangers in recent years, it's surprising that some users of social media networks are not more careful when it comes to "friending" or connecting with people online. But trusting others seems to come naturally to many of us.

The *Consumer Reports* survey also found that many social network users naively and routinely post their personal information and that of their children. For example, 26 percent of parents using Facebook had potentially exposed their children to predators by posting their photos and names. According to the survey, in 25 percent of households with Facebook accounts, users were unaware of or didn't use Facebook's privacy controls.

In order to protect themselves, online users must learn to ignore messages from strangers who ask for settings, passwords, or personal information.

With social media, there are few editors, and hardly anyone seems to corroborate the "facts" before posting them. Tweets and retweets aren't fact-checked. Social media are neutral technological tools that don't care if you are spreading lies. For example, during the riots in London in August 2011, James Cridland of Media UK found that Twitter wasn't reliable as a source for his articles and that even mainstream media weren't as reliable as he would have hoped:

> On the map, I asked people to get in contact with a verifiable source. It's surprising how many people think that a photograph or a video is verifiable: one compelling video sent to me last night was captioned "riots in Liverpool", but was actually from Woolwich in London. Surprising, too, how "a friend told me" was deemed reliable enough to pass on to me (it wasn't reliable enough for me to post.)
>
> It's curious how few people know how to check whether the news they're being told is verifiable.[7]

In Chapter 1, Meg Smith takes us through the world of Facebook, Myspace, Twitter, and other social networks, and points out the dangers of interacting online.

Identity Theft

By now you know not to post updates on Facebook about leaving your home unoccupied during your vacation. But it's more complicated than that. You also shouldn't post children's birth dates, your mother's maiden name, and other data requested when filling out all of those networking site quizzes. Not only are burglars looking to steal your china and furniture, they would also like to steal your identity and wipe out your lifetime savings.

According to the Privacy Rights Clearinghouse, a nonprofit consumer group, more than 347 million records containing sensitive information have been compromised in the U.S. since 2005. In March 2010, identity data on 3.3 million people with student loans was stolen, potentially affecting up to 5 percent of all federal student-loan borrowers:

> Names, addresses, Social Security numbers and other personal data on borrowers were stolen from the St. Paul, Minn., headquarters of Educational Credit Management Corp., a nonprofit guarantor of federal student loans, during the weekend of March 20–21, according to the company ... ECMC said the stolen information was on a portable media device. "It was simple, old-fashioned theft," said ECMC spokesman Paul Kelash. "It was not a hacker incident."[8]

This is not an isolated episode. Cynthia Hetherington spells it out in Chapter 2, offering tips and advice geared toward protecting your privacy and preventing identity theft.

Race and Religion

So-called hate sites target the fears people have of those who are different from them. Subtle or not, such sites are subversive. For me, the eye-opener came when I first saw www.martinlutherking.org, which gets traffic from teachers in schools, librarians teaching online users, and—unfortunately—many junior high school students in January of each year who are writing essays about Dr. King and who have yet to learn the lessons of this book. Factually correct, the site is also misleading, referring viewers to suggested readings by white supremacists.

Unfortunately, this phenomenon is not limited to the now-familiar www.martinlutherking.org.

Email messages spread virally, carrying rumors that stretch the limits of believability. Among the rumors listed as false on Snopes.com: that one should send an email to a particular address to protest the depiction of Jesus as a homosexual in an upcoming film; that Alabama redefined the value of pi to 3 to keep more in line with Biblical precepts; that a particular atheist has petitioned the Federal Communications Commission (petition number 2493) to stop the Gospel from being read over U.S. airwaves; that Snapple, Marlboro, and Timberland are all owned by the Ku Klux Klan; that American troops serving overseas are wearing uniforms made by a company owned by the Ku Klux Klan; and that designer Tommy Hilfiger announced on a talk show that he didn't want Asians or blacks buying his clothing.

Even computer games are now in on the act. In the free online video game *Border Patrol*, players aim and shoot at undocumented Mexicans crossing the Rio Grande River, with the goal of killing as many as possible. That's an intentionally bland description.

Canadian organization Media Awareness Network explains hatred in this way:

> Most definitions of hate focus on the ways in which hate-mongers see entire groups of people as the "Other." For example, U.S.-based tolerance.org argues that "All hate groups have beliefs or practices that attack or malign *an entire class of people*, typically for their immutable characteristics." … Canadian communications scholar Karim Karim points out that the "Other" is one of a number of human archetypes common to all cultures. When people transfer their fears and hatred to the "Other," the targeted group becomes less than human. Hate-mongers can then "justify" acts of violence and degradation because they have denied the humanity of their victims.[9]

In Chapter 3, Eli Edwards shows us how to identify these hate sites and rumors for what they actually are.

Ecommerce Fraud

How can you be scammed? Let me count the ways. Or at least here are a few ecommerce scams that you may not have thought of before. More than a few use social media tools to accomplish their goals.

According to CyberSource Corp., which processes credit cards for online merchants, the amount lost by North American merchants to fraud in 2010 was just under 1 percent: approximately $2.7 billion, a decline from $3.3 billion in 2009. (U.K. merchants saw an uptick in their fraud rate from 1.6 percent to 1.9 percent).[10] While there has been some progress in thwarting criminals defrauding online merchants, this type of commercial fraud is still commonplace, international in scope, and involved with merchandise of all kinds.

In a federal lawsuit brought to court in 2008, a woman in Olympia, Washington, was sentenced to 2 years in prison for conspiracy to commit bank, wire, and mail fraud.[11] Her crime? Helping criminals in Lagos, Nigeria, carry out a phony check-cashing scam. Other, similar cases have been filed that shed light on the scope of this activity, such as the 2010 criminal case *USA v. Svechinskaya et al*,[12] which focused on the use of "mules": those who are recruited to open bank accounts under false names and transfer stolen funds into accounts in Eastern Europe.

There are a variety of methods that criminals employ to part you from your money. Pay attention to the way you do business and shop on the internet, and take the advice offered by Ben Fractenberg in Chapter 4.

Information Warfare and Cybersecurity

In 2010, a computer worm named Stuxnet was discovered attacking certain types of Siemens industrial control computers used to manage electrical power grids, nuclear plants, and oil pipelines. It appeared in many countries, including India, Indonesia, China, and Iran, though its origins remain elusive. There has been speculation that the worm was designed specifically to attack Iranian computers used to develop nuclear weapons. However, the story gets ramped up a bit with some deeper skulduggery. In September 2010, news spread that the Israeli government was behind the worm and that it was subversively targeting the heavily secretive Iranian nuclear project. All this was based on the fact that one of the many files in the code was named Myrtus. The suggestion was that the name refers to the Persian Jewish queen, Esther—from the Bible's Old Testament—and that only an Israeli would name a file this way.

Others believe the name was intended to mislead the world into thinking the worm was created by Israel. Either way, there are serious implications when one country or religious group is accused of such behavior, and the intrigue continues. In August 2011, the *New York Times* reported that Chinese computers were the targets of nearly 500,000 cyberattacks in 2010.[13] According to the National Computer Network Emergency Response Coordination Center of China, almost half of the threats originated outside China and used Trojan Horse malware. Many originated in the U.S. No longer just spy vs. spy, this is the dangerous realm of information warfare as it evolves in the nonphysical world, described in considerable detail by Deborah Liptak in Chapter 5. She also explains the technologies of online deception and misinformation in Appendix B.

Political Shenanigans

In July 2010, news releases seemingly sent from the offices of U.S. senators Dianne Feinstein, Frank Lautenberg, and Patrick Leahy announced that each had died of liver cancer. The releases carried correct contact information and appeared at first to be sent from the proper URL for each senator's office. Only upon closer investigation was it revealed that they were fakes. Fortunately, the story that was carried on television and in major newspapers was the one about the hoaxes, not that the senators had died. But in the meantime, the misinformation had spread far and wide on the internet.

It gets more serious than rumors lasting less than one news cycle. There is subtlety and innuendo in many of the sites and advertisements on the internet that cleverly misleads readers. Things are taken out of context and then spread as the whole truth. In one of the most positive developments to come from the ubiquity of immediate online communication, it is now possible to counter viral political misinformation almost as soon as the false claims originate. Several media organizations and some televised Sunday morning conversation shows have instituted routine fact-checking of political sites and on-air pundits. Others joined forces with news fact-checker PolitiFact.

com to cover state elections and candidates. (PolitiFact.com has a "truth-o-meter" with one category named Pants on Fire.) The 2012 election cycle coverage features swift fact-checking of candidates' ads and speeches by both their opponents and by media organizations. The *New York Times* publishes a feature called Fact Check that serves the same purpose as PolitiFact.com; for example, it ran a Fact Check the day after the Iowa Caucus debates in August 2011.[14]

In Chapter 6, Laura Gordon-Murnane elaborates on the world of political "gotcha" and what remedies have been created to debunk that intentionally misleading information.

Charity Scams

It seems that with each new natural disaster there are opportunities to get scammed by nonexistent charities with compelling websites. Whether in the aftermath of Hurricane Katrina in 2005 or the earthquake that hit Haiti in 2010, or the earthquake and tsunami that devastated Japan in 2011, dozens if not hundreds of organizations claim to work on behalf of victims in dire need of materials and money to reconstruct their homes and their lives. Often, these requests tear at our heartstrings, but beware of "opportunities" to donate toys to children in need or to help raise money for breast cancer and other medical research. The useful Snopes.com debunks sites such as those claiming that purchasing Excedrin will help raise funds for Toys for Tots, that Merck will donate to cancer research if you purchase a particular bracelet, or that cellular service providers are raising money for the Susan G. Komen Foundation in support of breast cancer research. In Chapter 7, Craig Thompson shows how you can identify such scams and where to go for dependable sources to evaluate online charitable organizations.

Evaluating Websites

Just as we use electricity without thinking about how it is generated and transmitted to our light switches and sockets, we now use the internet without thinking about the mechanics of how data reaches our screens. In the same way that we carefully avoid being electrocuted, we must be careful not to get scammed, or worse. Amber Benham's guide to evaluating websites in Appendix A should go a long way in helping you avoid being misdirected while traveling the information superhighway.

According to a study by the Pew Internet & American Life Project, 77 percent of Americans were using the internet as of December 2010, a huge number no matter what baseline is used.[15] Many homes have high-speed connections. Many public locations offer free wireless access. Mobile devices such as cell phones connect online. Facebook, Myspace, Twitter, and LinkedIn have become popular social media sites. The internet is no longer just for techies; it's gone mainstream.

Much has changed since my earlier book, *Web of Deception: Misinformation on the Internet*, was published in 2002, yet much remains the same. Intentional misinformation is still all over the internet. Examples abound for every one of the topics covered in *Web of Deceit*, and it's a moving target. Each time I speak with friends about this subject, I get more examples of sites that pose problems or present data in misleading ways. All of this information may not still be online as you read this, but it was at one time. The Wayback Machine introduced by Brewster Kahle in October 2001 (www.archive.org) has captured these sites if they are not still viewable at the URLs cited. There are also references to lawsuits and legal proceedings in most chapters. It is possible that appeals and other procedures have overturned or modified these decisions, but they are accurate as we go to press.

A word about the contributed chapters and their authors: First, because the topics do not all fit in neat categories, you can expect some overlap in coverage. In addition, as with any contributed volume, the writing style will vary from one chapter to the next. As the editor, I've attempted to honor each contributor's voice while at the same time trying to present a unified work. Stylistic differences aside, one of my jobs has been to ensure that the research and reporting are of a consistently high caliber. I hope you'll feel that I succeeded.

Unfortunately, *Web of Deceit* will not fix what is broken. It will not identify all of the dangerous or misleading information out there. It will not change everyone's online behavior. But in publishing the book, it is our goal to help you be more alert to charity scams, identity theft, ecommerce fraud, and other criminal activities when using websites and social media tools. It is our goal that you become more aware of subversive activities involving computer worms, political operatives, and charlatans of all stripes and colors. We hope you will learn some valuable lessons and use that knowledge to help others avoid falling victim to misinformation and manipulation in this remarkable digital age we live in.

To all of our readers, we wish you a safe journey.

Endnotes

1. Copyright of BBDO Advertising Agency.

2. Enron Chief Executive Kenneth Lay died of heart failure in July 2006 before he could be sentenced. His conviction was thrown out since his death prevented him from appealing the verdict.

3. *United States of America, ex rel. et al. v. GlaxoSmithKline Holdings (Americas) Inc. et al.*, Case 1:04-cv-10375-JLT filed in United States District Court, Massachusetts District Court in Boston on February 27, 2004.

4. Gretchen Morgenson, "Raters Ignored Proof of Unsafe Loans, Panel Is Told," *New York Times*, September 26, 2010, accessed May 17, 2011, www.nytimes.com/2010/09/27/business/27ratings.html?scp=1&sq=raters%20ignored%20proof&st=cset.

5. "Online Exposure," ConsumerReports.org, June 2011, accessed July 28, 2011, www.consumerreports.org/cro/magazine-archive/2011/june/electronics-computers/state-of-the-net/online-exposure/index.htm.

6. "Nashua Police Announce Burglary Ring Arrests," Nashua Police Department, September 8, 2010, accessed May 17, 2011, www.nashuapd.com/PR/11%20st%20Burglary%20investigation.pdf.

7. James Cridland, "What I Learned Mapping the London Riots," paidContent.org, August 9, 2011, accessed September 7, 2011, www.paidcontent.org/article/419-what-i-learned-mapping-the-london-riots.

8. Mary Pilon, "Data Theft Hits 3.3 Million Borrowers," WSJ.com, March 29, 2010, accessed May 17, 2011, online.wsj.com/article/SB10001424052702304434404575150024174102954.html.

9. "What Is Hate?," Media Awareness Network, accessed May 17, 2011, www.media-awareness.ca/english/issues/online_hate/what_is_hate.cfm.

10. "Merchants Hit Back at eCommerce Fraud," CyberSource Corp., accessed May 17, 2011, www.cybersource.com/news_and_events/view.php?page_id=1798.

11. *United States of America v. Edna Fiedler*, Case 3:08-cr-05032-BHS-001 filed in United States District Court, Western District of Washington in Tacoma on January 16, 2008.

12. *United States of America v. Svechinskaya et al.*, Case 1:10-mj-02137-UA-1 filed in United States District Court, Southern District of New York in Manhattan on September 28, 2010.

13. Edward Wong, "China: Agency Reports 500,000 Cyberattacks in 2010," *New York Times*, August 9, 2011, accessed September 7, 2011, www.nytimes.com/2011/08/10/world/asia/10briefs-cyberattacks.html?_r=1&ref=todayspaper.

14. Michael Cooper, "Fact Check: The Republican Debate," The Caucus, August 11, 2011, accessed September 7, 2011, www.thecaucus.blogs.nytimes.com/2011/08/11/fact-check-the-republican-debate.

15. For Pew internet, broadband, and cell phone statistics, visit www.pewinternet.org/Static-Pages/Trend-Data/Whos-Online.aspx.

"I just feel fortunate to live in a world with so much disinformation at my fingertips."

CHAPTER 1

Social Media and Intentional Misinformation

Meg Smith

In October 2006, a whirlwind online romance came to a crashing halt. Four weeks after a stranger named Josh Evans wooed 13-year-old Megan Meier on Myspace with heartfelt messages and flirtatious compliments, he turned on her, saying that he didn't want to be her friend anymore. According to prosecutors, he said that "the world would be a better place without [her] in it."[1] In despair and embarrassed that other online friends seemed to know about Josh's rejection instantly, Megan committed suicide in her bedroom with her parents just a few steps away inside the house.[2] A police investigation revealed that Josh Evans actually did not exist: He was the creation of an adult neighbor, Lori Drew, who used "him" to spy on Megan after she stopped being friends with Drew's daughter. But the stunt quickly devolved from spying to something even more malicious: Drew gave three teenage girls access to the secret profile, and they used it to insult and reject Megan through the imaginary avatar better known as Josh Evans. Drew was prosecuted in what the *New York Times* called the country's first cyberbullying trial.[3] Though Drew was found guilty of fraud in the emotionally charged trial, she was cleared on appeal. The appeals court found that violating Myspace's terms of use did not meet the legal definition of fraud.

Though Drew was ultimately cleared, the unprecedented trial left parents, school officials, prosecutors, and the media with the same disturbing thought: Deception on social networking sites is so easy, even a parent can do it.

As with art forgers and currency counterfeiters, the scammers who operate on social networking sites try to create messages that convince viewers they are looking at something authentic and trustworthy. But on social networking sites, where hundreds of millions of users create billions of pages of content by posting their own photos and messages, there are few monitors or regulators watching for fakes. Users have to be the curators of their own friends and make informed judgments about which messages to reply to and which links to click on. Those who fail to spot a phony profile or message can suffer consequences ranging from embarrassment to identity theft. But in the most extreme cases, such as what happened to Megan, when a victim's involvement with a deceiver crosses over into the real world, the consequences can be fatal.

Social Behavior

In the art world, the best way to spot a forgery is to know as much as possible about the original. Similarly, one of the best defenses against online deception is to understand how each of the most popular social networking sites in the U.S. is supposed to be used.

Social networking sites are essentially designed to digitally re-create users' social networks in real life; they bring together a user's friends, family, colleagues, neighbors, and schoolmates and give them a forum to communicate. As social media moved from being a hobby for the technologically adept to a popular pastime for the average internet user, it gained appeal in the commercial sector. Now, social networks also frequently encourage users to share their favorite products, news outlets, celebrities, and politicians.

For more than a decade, the rapid adoption of web-based applications has blurred the line between the internet and the real world. Now, the real world is online, too. Offline, our social networks are more than just the people we love and trust. Beyond their inner layers are people with whom we don't socialize: the strangers who cross our paths every day and who are also online. While most of them are using social media legitimately, some are eager to take advantage of unwitting victims.

Online scammers need their victims to trust them just long enough to fall for a scheme: They offer victims a link to click, a phony message to forward to associates, or a convincing sob story so victims wire the scammer money. Other scams are based on outright fraud. Just as email spammers have always tried to give their solicitations a sense of credibility by crafting return addresses and subject lines that appear to be from someone the victim knows, social media predators also camouflage themselves, sometimes going as far as to hijack the accounts of real people to target their friends list.

In a chilling demonstration of how often this can happen, MIT's *Technology Review* reported in May 2010 that hijacked Twitter accounts were for sale on Russian hacker forums in lots of 1,000. The price varied from $100 to $200 per lot, based on how many followers the account had when it was hijacked; more followers ideally meant more people who could be tricked into thinking a scammer's message was actually coming from someone they knew.[4] That same month, internet security researchers at VeriSign reported that a criminal broker attempted to sell 1.5 million hijacked Facebook accounts in February, offering them in lots of 1,000 with a similar sliding price scale based on the number of friends.[5] If thousands of accounts change hands in transactions such as these two, it's hard to imagine how many hijacked accounts there are overall.

This chapter describes some of the most common forms of deception on Facebook, Myspace, and Twitter, three of the most popular social media sites in the U.S., and explains how to apply the lessons learned to other sites across the social web.

Facebook

Facebook is the second most popular website in the world, behind only Google in the number of unique visitors it receives.[6] Facebook has more than 750 million users, who spend an average of about 30 minutes per day on the site.[7] This means if Facebook were a country, it would be the third largest in the world behind China and India.

It is almost impossible to overestimate Facebook's reach and impact on internet users today. Google's advertising division, Ad Planner, estimates that 35 percent of web users visit Facebook each month.[8] Corporations hire firms to monitor comments on the site for signs of customer unrest and fiercely guard their brand names for signs of infringement or misuse on fan pages.[9] When consumers are happy, the groundswell of support that Facebook brings to an organization is nearly priceless. *Saturday Night Live* was rewarded with its fourth-highest viewership in 23 years when it acquiesced to a Facebook-driven campaign to have Betty White host an episode. It was the only time that year the NBC comedy show attracted as many 18- to 29-year-old viewers as a typical episode of *American Idol*.[10]

Negative attention can be equally devastating when consumers turn against a product and use Facebook to announce their concerns. Proctor & Gamble Co. rushed to address a 10,000-member group called "Pampers bring back the OLD CRUISERS/SWADDLERS," which alleged that the company's new "Dry Max" diaper material was causing unusual diaper rashes for babies. The Facebook group drew the attention of the media and thousands of parents before the Consumer Product Safety Commission was able to verify that there was no connection between the product and the rashes.[11]

When Facebook itself makes a change users don't like or understand, the consequences are even greater. In December 2009 and May 2010, Facebook changed its privacy settings so more of a user's information would be displayed by default, and some information would be permanently displayed for the first time. The uproar that followed had as much to do with Facebook's enormous userbase as with the changes themselves. Facebook had relaxed many privacy settings in the past, but none received as much attention in the media as these. Previous changes included the 2006 introduction of the News Feed, which reports on every action taken by a user's friends; a brief and much-despised partnership in 2007 with a service that broadcast what users bought online to their friends list; and the historic decision that year to allow profiles to be indexed by Google and other search engines. Though those changes were arguably more significant and made Facebook into what it is today, changes going forward will affect hundreds of millions more members. Many of Facebook's newest users are former social-media holdouts who avoided earlier services such as Myspace, Friendster, and Orkut and are experiencing the tension between privacy and interactivity that comes with cultivating an identity online for the first time.

All of Facebook's privacy changes are remarkable, given how cloistered users were when the service began. Mark Zuckerberg created Faccbook in 2004 as a dynamic yearbook for his fellow Harvard students. A month later, he opened Facebook to students from three other Ivy League schools. By the following year, students from 800 universities were permitted to sign up with their branded ".edu" email addresses.[12] Facebook organized these users into silos, allowing them to view all the profiles of users within their own college's network but not view users in other networks. In 2006, workplaces that supported their own branded email addresses were given networks on Facebook's site, allowing employees from more than 1,000 companies to join the service. Though the service was becoming more popular among these self-contained groups, the general public still had no way to join. The guiding ethic of Facebook's early years—you had to belong to a corporate or educational network in order to join—permeated the rest of the site as well. Instead of choosing a username, members had to use their real full names at signup. The network they were assigned to immediately revealed their school affiliation or employer to other users. Though Facebook could not verify other details users added to their profiles, the use of real names and clustering people together from the same school or employer had the effect of encouraging early users to behave online as they do in the real world: to be themselves. The very fact that members belonged to an institution of higher learning or worked for an employer that had issued them email addresses meant that users constituted an upscale demographic. Especially in the 2000s, branded email networks were usually backed by an expensive computer infrastructure, and users were often technologically more adept than the general population. Therefore, Facebook was a service that appealed to savvy internet users and socially integrated individuals. The real opportunities for mischief didn't begin until the end of 2006, when Facebook opened its doors to everyone else.

Impersonation Scams on Facebook

Social networks on Facebook are identity-based. Because people are using their real names and are organized into affiliation networks, they tend to know many of the people on their friends list in real life. So a hijacked account is valuable to thieves because trust between users has already been established, which makes a scam that much easier to carry out.

Computer worms are malicious programs that replicate and spread through a network once they have infected a host computer. On Facebook, the worm spreads through a user's *social* network. The highly effective Koobface worm, which first appeared in 2008, has never been completely eradicated. It takes the form of a message in a user's inbox from someone in his network who has already been infected. The message asks whether the user has seen himself in a new online video; the Trojan friend then appears to be offering a link of the video to the user. If the user clicks on the link, he will be diverted from Facebook.com to a website that will install malware on his computer. Once unleashed, Koobface changes the victim's Facebook password and sends the message to everyone on his friends list. It scans the computer for credit card information and searches saved cookies for passwords to other social networking sites such as Twitter and Myspace. It then sends the Trojan message to friends on those sites, too. Facebook worms that followed Koobface have tended to masquerade as videos embedded on profile walls or in messages. (For more information on Koobface, see Chapter 4.)

Genuine videos that are embedded in a message or on a wall will play directly from the Facebook page once clicked. If they are legitimate, these videos will not take you to an outside website. Watchful users will often notice details that reveal fraudulent links before they've even clicked on them. One is the tone: Often written with grammatical errors or crafted to read like a text message from a teenager, the message will often not match the personality of the friend who allegedly sent the message. The other is the subject matter: If the video seems to be in poor taste, or if the person offering the video is not known to make videos, it's best to call or email the friend and make sure the message is real. As described earlier in the chapter, these hijacked accounts have monetary value to hackers, who can then use them to unleash new worms in the future.

Since 2009, a growing number of scams involve guessing an individual's password and making personal, one-on-one appeals to friends to send money, claiming the hacked user was robbed or detained while visiting a foreign country. Because so many people use the same password for accounts all over the web, scammers often find victims by hacking less-sophisticated websites, stealing email addresses and passwords from the weaker sites, and then testing to see if the credentials work on Facebook as well. The scheme requires a sizable time investment to deduce the passwords, learn details about the victims' families that can be used to make the appeal for money more convincing, and use the chat feature in Facebook to persuade friends to send money. It works often enough to be worth the effort. The Associated Press reported that a woman in Missouri wired $4,000 to London after someone posing as an immigration official called her and said a Facebook friend of hers had been detained after losing her passport.[13] For cases like this, attempting to reach the friend through other means before sending the money would defeat the scam. To protect Facebook accounts from being hijacked by scammers, internet security experts recommend using a different password for each of your web-based accounts.[14] At the very least, create unique passwords for Facebook and email, which are currently the main targets of similar scams.

And then there is a type of scam that goes beyond a victim's login credentials and money to cause physical and psychological harm: blackmail and sexual coercion. Remarkably, examples of blackmail have increased in recent years, tied to the rise in "sexting" among young people, and the predators are sometimes barely older than their victims. While Facebook accounts for some of the examples because it makes the victims easy to track down and threaten in real life, several major social networking services have been the settings for blackmail.

In late 2009, a 19-year-old Wisconsin man pled guilty to sexual assault after he posed as a teenage girl on Facebook and tricked 31 teenage boys into sending him nude photos of themselves. He then threatened to send the photos to everyone in the boys' high school networks on Facebook if they did not agree to meet with him and perform sexual acts. Half of them met his demands, and their sexual assaults became the basis of his arrest and prosecution.[15] In Ottawa the next year, an 18-year-old man whom the media dubbed the "Webcam Puppeteer" blackmailed 22 adult women and girls as young as 14 years old into undressing in front of their webcams at home while men paid to watch them over the internet. He had convinced them to send him nude photos of themselves in exchange for thousands of dollars, but instead of paying them, he threatened to send the photos to relatives and coworkers on their friends lists if they did not perform more acts under his command. In his confession, the man told police that one of his victims said she wanted to kill herself as she followed his orders over her webcam. Others cried throughout their remote-controlled sexual assaults.[16]

Social Games on Facebook

Facebook users spend more than 700 billion minutes per month on the site, and a large amount of that time is spent using Facebook applications. The support invested in these apps behind the scenes is as enormous as the userbase: One million developers have built more than 500,000 applications.[17] Just as users are expected to adhere to Facebook's terms of use, developers have policies they must adhere to as well. However, both are only as good as their enforcement, and it takes sharp-eyed industry experts to notice when the rules are not strong enough to protect users from deception.

In fall 2009, TechCrunch editor Michael Arrington published a series of articles exploring the "dark side" of social network game developers, including Zynga, maker of the wildly popular *Farmville*, *Mafia Wars*, and *Texas Hold Em' Poker* applications.[18] More than 100 million Facebook users play Zynga's games, which are free to access and play through Facebook, but they require in-game virtual credits in order to progress to more advanced levels. Users have the option to buy in-game credits with a credit card, or they can sign up for trial offers of products and services to earn credits. Arrington demonstrated that many of the trials are actually opt-out programs that result in users receiving unwanted merchandise. Users then have to return this merchandize while reversing large charges or tracking down the service provider months later to stop a recurring charge from being added to cell phone and credit card bills.[19] After Arrington's exposé attracted the attention of class action lawyers and the media, Myspace announced a change in its developer agreement that prohibited opt-out structured offers. Facebook announced 6 months later that it had entered into a 5-year agreement to keep Zynga's games on its site and stated that it had plans to roll out its own virtual-credit-granting service called Facebook Credits.

Facebook is much the same as the colleges it served in its early days. Tucked inside its massive fortress are vast numbers of new people to get to know and interact with, and countless activities to enjoy and to share with friends. The à la carte privacy settings and restricted networks that users can join give Facebook the feeling of exclusivity;

the use of real names engenders at least the idea of civility. But as with any college campus filled with new temptations and responsibilities, dangers lurk here as they do anywhere. It's important to remain vigilant and help young people getting online for the first time develop awareness of their surroundings and a healthy dose of skepticism.

Myspace

Myspace was one of the earliest social networking websites to achieve mass success. Though it has since been eclipsed by Facebook, it still claims 100 million users[20] and continues to be in the top 100 most popular websites in the U.S.[21] When Myspace was founded in 2004, its creators aspired to make it the "MTV of the internet,"[22] connecting musicians to their fans and allowing listeners to sample songs and videos, to network with other fans, and to get updates from the artists they chose to follow. By going after popular music lovers, Myspace attracted mainstream teenagers and young adults to its site in droves.

Myspace has always been free to join and imposes no restrictions other than the federally mandated requirement that users be at least 13 years old, which means that people can sign up with as little as a free, anonymous Hotmail or Yahoo! account. The very low technological barrier means average users—often the last to try new web-based applications and services—can embrace the service and become comfortable with it quickly. For example, it became such a popular way for military families to keep in touch with personnel stationed overseas that the Pentagon banned its use in May 2007 to ease the strain it was putting on military bandwidth.[23]

The relaxed barriers to membership also extend inside the service after signup, leading to an atmosphere where it is difficult to know what is real and what is not. Users can fill out as much or as little of their profile as they want without ever having to verify that answers are true. Myspace allows users to offer numerous details about their education, employment, age, income, and interests, and even allows them to declare their status within an industry as part of its "networking" feature. This raises expectations that the information provided will shed light on the person who created the profile, but it also offers opportunities for deception. After all, who knows how many

Myspace users have been unable to resist selecting the option that displays their income as "$250,000 and Higher"?

Tom Anderson, Myspace's co-founder, intended for these information fields to be unmoderated. According to Julie Angwin's *Stealing MySpace: The Battle to Control the Most Popular Website in America*, Anderson created Myspace as a rival to the social networking site Friendster after Friendster's managers began deleting profiles that impersonated famous people or fictional characters.[24] When Myspace was founded, online anonymity was still a sacred value among denizens of the web. As Anderson saw it, deception—whether posing as a cartoon character or a highly compensated high school student—is a form of anonymity that users should be free to choose for themselves.[25]

But Myspace also built a counterweight to the temptation to deceive: The information fields are connected, so everyone who lists the same hometown, high school, or employer can find each other easily. Most users typically want to connect with people they actually know and want to be recognized by those people when they request their friendship online. Therefore, income declarations aside, legitimate Myspace users have an incentive to be honest on biographical details they have in common with their friends: location, schools attended, and employers, in particular. There are also some fields that users cannot alter; the email address used at signup is searchable by default, so the profile can be found by acquaintances, and the date of last login is always visible. Users can also take advantage of an option to make their profile appear in search results if their full name is searched, without displaying the name in their profile.

Person-to-Person Scams on Myspace

Remember the tragic case of Megan Meier's suicide, triggered in part by the cruel rejection of the imaginary Josh Evans? The government noted in its case against Lori Drew that Josh Evans's profile was unique in several ways, requiring a creative explanation by the profile's forgers. No high school was listed on the profile, possibly out of fear that Megan might check to see if her new friend really went to the school the scammers chose. Josh Evans also had no other friends when he reached out to her. According to the prosecutors, Josh Evans explained to Megan that he didn't have any friends or school affiliation because he was homeschooled and had just moved into town.[26]

As implausible as that excuse was, there was one most telling detail of his profile: The Josh Evans account had been created the same day he reached out to her. Lori Drew and her teenage accomplices were so eager to start spying on Megan that they didn't take time to develop their page into one that would appear more credible. And 13-year-old Megan, so flattered by the attention, was not suspicious enough to wonder how a handsome boy with no friends or school affiliation managed to find her in less than a day on a site with more than 100 million profiles.

A profile on any social networking site that has been created for a single purpose, like the Josh Evans profile or a spam profile hawking spyware, will probably be used very quickly by its designer. In personal scams such as the one carried out against Megan Meier, a designer may be overeager to get started. In spam-related scams, designers will need to approach hundreds if not thousands of people before they find one who will fall for the deception, and they have to work quickly to have an impact before the profile is reported and banned for violating the particular site's antispam rules.

Any time a stranger approaches a user online and requests some kind of action from the user, it is wise to be suspicious. The safest action a user can take when approached by a stranger on Myspace is to ignore the stranger completely. It's no ruder to do so than to ignore a honking car horn while walking on the sidewalk. If advice to ignore all strangers seems too restrictive, pay careful attention to what the stranger is asking. It is one thing to have a conversation about a common interest, but if the stranger needs you to send money, meet in the real world, follow a link to an external website, or take any other action, beware. A total stranger shouldn't need you to do anything.

As with the infamous Nigerian email scam offering respondents millions of dollars if they wire modest fees to the scammers, the most effective and devastating deceptions on Myspace try to overcome users' natural suspicions by offering something too good to resist. In the case of Megan Meier, who had just changed schools, the Josh Evans profile preyed upon her loneliness. In other recent examples, the temptations came in the form of well-paying jobs.

An arrest in April 2010 by the Palm Beach County Sheriff's office demonstrates just how compelling an unsolicited offer on Myspace can be and how effectively a scammer's pressure to act quickly can overwhelm victims' common sense. The suspect was charged with luring two women into meeting him face-to-face with the promise of finding them well-paying jobs. He browsed Myspace for profiles belonging to women located near him and contacted potential victims with an offer for an $18 per hour receptionist job that came with full medical benefits and matching contributions to a 401(k) account. Posing to the first victim as an employer named "Joaquin" and to the second 4 months later as "Junior," the suspect told them he needed to fill the vacancy very quickly and was about to leave town. He pressured each of them to meet him late at night at a gas station in Palm Beach. Once there, he persuaded them to let him borrow their cell phones and to sit in his car, setting them up for the crime: abduction and sexual assault. The first victim, attacked in January, told police she complained about the meeting conditions, calling it "unprofessional" to meet at a gas station late at night, but nonetheless she felt she couldn't afford to pass up the opportunity.[27]

One-to-Many Scams on Myspace

Deceptive messages known as phishing attacks, designed to get users to click on a poisoned link, often take the form of comments left on a user's Myspace profile. Scammers posing as up-and-coming musicians post links to their phony fan sites, attractive models attempt to lure victims to dating sites no one has ever heard of, and some offers even masquerade as solicitations to donate to disaster relief. The URL written in the solicitation is almost never the actual website linked to in the message's HTML code. Fortunately, most modern web browsers will display the real URL at the bottom of the browser window if the user places the cursor over the link. If the real URL and the displayed URL do not match, the link is not safe.

Most phishing attacks have one thing in common: They are trying to lure users off Myspace and onto a website where the rest of the scam takes place. Once drawn away from Myspace's fairly regulated environment, victims are either tricked into giving away personal passwords and other information to a website designed to look like a trusted service such as Twitter or Gmail, or their computers are hijacked by malware that makes escape nearly impossible.

In 2006, the Federal Trade Commission (FTC) reached a settlement in federal court with Odysseus Marketing in which Odysseus agreed to stop sending offers for a free peer-to-peer file sharing service disguised to look as though they had come from Myspace users. The software was laced with hidden programs that hobbled infected computers with pop-up ads, transmitted personal data back to the company, and hijacked the victims' internet search results, replacing the real sites with links to sites controlled by the company. In 2009, the company's principal and his associates were held in contempt of court. They were ordered to refund more than $500,000 that they had collected from a new phishing attack against Myspace users, having violated the agreement in the original settlement to stop using deceptive methods to gather personal user data. According to the FTC, this scam "redirected users to [advertising] websites other than those they chose to visit by 'pagejacking' them ... and disabled users' web-browser navigation controls, a practice known as 'mousetrapping,' that allows scammers to take charge of which sites consumers visit."[28]

The best way to repel phishing messages is to adjust Myspace settings so that only friends can send messages and post comments on a user's profile. The settings are accessible by choosing My Account and then Spam, and looking for two categories: Messages and Comments. Under Messages, the most restrictive setting is to leave both boxes unchecked, which has the effect of prohibiting nonfriends from communicating with you. Under Comments, the most restrictive setting is to check the box next to "Only friends can add comments to my blog."

Another way to make a profile less attractive to spammers is to go into the Privacy setting in My Account and deactivate the option to "Show people when I am online." Spammers and con artists tend to target people who are online in the hopes of getting an instant reaction. Myspace also lists the profiles of people who are "Online Now!" at the top of search results, which is how spammers usually find them.

Twitter

Compared with many other social sites, Twitter was an easy sell to internet users. The update field resembled Facebook's status box, the restriction on length gave it the feel of an instant messaging service, and the simplicity of its design made it an easy application to operate from mobile devices. At the time of this writing, Twitter is the 8th-most-popular website in the U.S. and growing at a rate of 460,000 new accounts per day.[29]

Though it is possible for users to protect their tweets from public view, Twitter is designed to be a crowdsourcing application that aggregates insights, opinions, and observations from people around the world. In many ways, crowdsourcing is antithetical to the author-itative, hierarchical presentation of information that civilization depended on before the rise of the social web. Twitter's impact comes not from the depth of individuals' expertise, but from the extraordi-nary loft given to ideas as they are spread by multitudes.

There have already been many examples of Twitter's power. Though Twitter allows messages up to 140 characters long, the tweet that made the service famous contained just one word, "Arrested," sent by 29-year-old James Buck on April 10, 2008.[30] The Berkeley journalism student was in Egypt interviewing protestors during a demonstration when police took him and his translator into custody. Tipped off to the tweet by Buck's friends, the University of California at Berkeley hired a lawyer for him and contacted the State Department.[31] Buck was freed the next day, and he devoted his Twitter account and his newfound celebrity to securing the release of his Egyptian-born translator, who was freed several months later.

The following year, Iranian supporters of the presidential candi-date Mir Hossein Mousavi relied on Twitter to announce protests against the disputed re-election of President Mahmoud Ahmadinejad and document police violence against protestors. But Iranians weren't using Twitter just to communicate with each other; the entire world was listening. Users following the original Iranian tweeters were attaching the hashtag *#IranRevolution* to the end of messages and forwarding them to their own followers, who would in turn forward them on to their followers. This way, one message was passed along to hundreds more people, and then seen again by thousands more who were searching Twitter for public posts with the hashtag *#IranRevolution*. This kept the ideas propagating even if Iranian authorities shut down certain Twitter accounts. As Iran expelled foreign media from the country and suppressed news of the demonstrations, protestors uploaded tweets and videos to YouTube, one of the world's few unbroken links to events happening inside the country. The State Department even asked Twitter to postpone a temporary shutdown for maintenance so it could continue to be used for communication.[32]

But with so many eyes on the hashtag *#IranRevolution* and no control over who could use it, misinformation began creeping into the stream. Rumors began spreading that YouTube was censoring videos of Iranian police brutality, and users began posting links to alternate video hosting sites. It's unknown whether these were altruistic suggestions by people who were quick to believe the rumors, or if they were opportunistic companies trying to lead viewers to their sites. Companies also began using *#IranRevolution* to advertise services where users could post comments anonymously to the web. Altruism and opportunism became difficult to separate. The stream became so choked with outsiders adding their own thoughts and ideas that Iranian demonstrators would have had trouble finding fresh information when searching for the hashtag *#IranRevolution*. They would have been better off following the tweets from people they trusted inside the country.

The State Department was not the only government agency watching Twitter's extraordinary usefulness during the Iran demonstrations.[33] The U.S. military's Defense Advanced Research Projects Agency (DARPA) put Twitter to the ultimate test 6 months later. DARPA designed a contest that would determine whether social networks could be mobilized for a real-world assignment. The contest was to see who could find 10 locations around the nation where giant red balloons had been placed, a task DARPA's analysts deemed nearly impossible to accomplish using current intelligence techniques.

Exploiting online social networks, it took the winning team less than 9 hours to complete this "impossible" task, obtaining the locations of five of the balloons on Twitter and the other five by tapping into an online network of 4,500 participants the team had built from scratch in 36 hours. But DARPA noted in its final report that the winning team had given itself an advantage by creating a "false report rejection strategy," anticipating that rival teams would launch disinformation campaigns on Twitter to plant false reports of balloons to throw off competitors.[34] Due to nationwide mainstream media coverage, there were also many well-meaning people who posted sightings of red balloons on Twitter, even though they weren't the right kind of balloons. The winning team located the five true Twitter balloon sightings by comparing IP addresses to the stated locations of the balloons, analyzing the photos for any signs of forgery, and dispatching spotters to verify the locations. Team members anticipated the need to weed out false reports, which ultimately contributed to their victory.

DARPA's conclusion about Twitter takes into account the site's best and worst traits: "The Challenge revealed how fast and dynamic Twitter can be as a responsive data source, but it also confirmed the inherent noise in tweet data streams as well as how difficult it is to extract the desired information."[35]

Across the Social Web

Facebook, Myspace, and Twitter are excellent laboratories for social scams because of their critical mass of users. Lessons learned from using these tools can be applied across the many Web 2.0 platforms that allow users to create their own content and interact with each other directly without moderation.

The Myspace employment scam has also taken place on Facebook, leading to the murder of an 18-year-old woman in Australia in 2010.[36] Variations of this scam involving identity theft instead of bodily injury are rampant on craigslist, where victims are duped into emailing their Social Security and bank account numbers to alleged employers who say they are hiring for work-at-home jobs. There are countless other types of scams on craigslist involving entreaties to ship products overseas and allow the buyer to pay for the goods electronically. Craigslist has one simple suggestion that will defeat nearly every scam on its site: "Deal locally with folks you can meet in person [and pay in cash]." Each city's homepage on craigslist has a guide called Avoid Scams & Fraud, containing this tip and many more.

The sexual blackmail scam described earlier is especially popular in the U.K. Because of this growing danger, recent policy shifts toward charging teenagers with distribution of child pornography to suppress "sexting" may backfire.[37] If children don't feel safe reporting this kind of blackmail and coercion to authorities when it happens, they could be as trapped in their blackmailers' orbits as children who have been trafficked into sexual slavery.

The bottom line is that people who want users to do something for them—click on a link, send them photos or money, watch a video, or meet them in real life—are probably scammers. Real online friends will probably be introduced by a mutual acquaintance or will share a common interest or hobby; they aren't likely to find a user on their own out of the blue. Real online friends will just want to talk; they won't take something from a user or ask them to leave the social networking site and visit other parts of the web. Most importantly, real friends take their time; there shouldn't be any pressure to act quickly.

Endnotes

1. "Government's Opposition to Defendant's Motion to Dismiss the Indictment for Vagueness," *United States v. Drew*, U.S. District Court for the Central District of California, 08-CR 582, filed August 12, 2008, 13.

2. Tamara Jones, "A Deadly Web of Deceit," *Washington Post*, January 10, 2008, C1.

3. Jennifer Steinhauer, "Woman Found Guilty in Web Fraud Tied to Suicide," *New York Times,* November 27, 2008, A25.

4. David Talbot, "For Sale: Thousands of Hacked Twitter Accounts," *Technology Review,* May 13, 2010, accessed May 18, 2011, technologyreview.com/web/25297.

5. Riva Richmond, "Stolen Facebook Accounts for Sale," *New York Times,* May 3, 2010, B3.

6. "Top Sites," Alexa: The Web Information Company, accessed May 18, 2011, www.alexa.com/topsites.

7. "Statistics," Facebook, accessed May 18, 2011, www.facebook.com/press/info.php?statistics.

8. "The 1000 Most-Visited Sites on the Web," DoubleClick Ad Planner by Google, accessed May 18, 2011, www.google.com/adplanner/static/top1000.

9. Robert L. Mitchell, "Scams & Shams: The Trouble With Social Networks," *ComputerWorld*, October 19, 2009, accessed July 17, 2011, www.computerworld.com/s/article/342446/Scams_Spams_Shams.

10. Bill Carter, "An Even Better Number for Betty White's 'SNL' Turn," *New York Times,* May 24, 2010, accessed May 18, 2011, mediadecoder.blogs.nytimes.com/2010/05/24/an-even-better-number-for-betty-whites-snl-turn.

11. Natasha Metzler, "Government Finds No Specific Connections Between Pampers Diapers With Dry Max and Diaper Rash," Associated Press, September 2, 2010, from Lexis Nexis, April 25, 2010.

12. "Company Timeline," Facebook, accessed May 18, 2011, www.facebook.com/press/info.php?timeline.

13. Betsy Taylor, "Facebook Scam Leads Mo. Woman to Wire $4k Abroad," Associated Press, September 2, 2009, from Lexis Nexis, April 25, 2010.

14. Theresa Payton, "Cyberscumbags Hijacking Social Media Accounts," Infosec Island, May 4, 2010, accessed May 18, 2011, www.infosecisland.com/blog view/3907-Cyberscumbags-Hijacking-Social-Media-Accounts.html.

15. Mike Johnson, "Stancl Is Convicted of Assault," *Milwaukee Journal Sentinel*, December 23, 2009, B1.

16. Matthew Pearson, "Sex, Lies and Webcams," *Ottawa Citizen*, May 5, 2010, A1.

17. "Statistics," Facebook.

18. Matt Burns, "Social Games: How the Big Three Make Millions," TechCrunch.com, October 26, 2009, accessed May 18, 2011, techcrunch.com/2009/10/26/social-games-how-the-big-three-make-millions.

19. Michael Arrington, "Scamville: The Social Gaming Ecosystem of Hell," TechCrunch.com, October 31, 2009, accessed May 18, 2011, techcrunch.com/2009/10/31/scamville-the-social-gaming-ecosystem-of-hell.

20. "Fact Sheet," Myspace, accessed July 17, 2011, www.myspace.com/pressroom/fact-sheet.

21. "Myspace.com," Alexa: The Web Information Company, accessed July 29, 2011, www.alexa.com/siteinfo/myspace.com

22. Julia Angwin, *Stealing MySpace: The Battle to Control the Most Popular Website in America* (New York: Random House, 2009), 104.

23. Pauline Jelinek, "Pentagon Issues New Policy on Social Networking," Associated Press, February 26, 2010, from Lexis Nexis, April 25, 2010. *Note:* The Pentagon restored Myspace access to military users in February 2010, concluding that banning Myspace had just driven traffic to other sites, resulting in no net gain of bandwidth.

24. Angwin, 55.

25. Ibid.

26. "Government's Opposition," *USA v. Drew*, 11–12.

27. Erika Pesantes, "Expert: Social Networking Sites Can Be Used to Lure Crime Victims," *South Florida Sun-Sentinel,* April 10, 2010, accessed July 17, 2011, articles.sun-sentinel.com/2010-04-08/news/fl-greenacres-rape-case-20100408_1_social-networking-victim-greenacres-man.

28. Federal Trade Commission, "Court Orders Internet Pagejackers to Return Ill-Gotten Gains," July 30, 2009, accessed May 18, 2011, www.ftc.gov/opa/2009/07/odysseus.shtm.

29. For statistics about Twitter, see www.alexa.com/siteinfo/twitter.com and business.twitter.com/basics/what-is-twitter, accessed July 17, 2011.

30. James Buck, Twitter, April 10, 2008, accessed May 18, 2011, twitter.com/james buck/status/786571964.

31. Mike Musgrove, "Held by Egyptian Authorities? Time to 'Tweet'," *Washington Post,* April 19, 2008, D1.

32. Matthew Lee, "Officials: Twitter Stayed Online for Iran Chaos," Associated Press, June 16, 2009, from Lexis Nexis, April 25, 2010.

33. Defense Advanced Research Projects Agency, *Darpa Network Challenge: Project Report,* February 16, 2010, 15, accessed May 18, 2011, networkchallenge. darpa.mil/ProjectReport.pdf. The report can also be viewed at www.eecs.harvard. edu/cs286r/papers/ProjectReport.pdf.

34. Ibid., 5.

35. Ibid., 14.

36. Elle Halliwell and Lisa Mayoh, "Facebook Teen Killed," *Sunday Telegraph,* May 16, 2010, from Lexis Nexis, March 29, 2010.

37. For example: Ed Anderson, "Ban on Juvenile 'Sexting' Approved; Teens Could Receive a Month in Jail," *Times-Picayune,* May 7, 2010, A2. For a discussion of attempts to loosen laws relating to sexting see Tamar Lewin, "Rethinking Sex Offender Laws for Youths Showing Off Online," *New York Times*, March 21, 2010, A1.

CHAPTER 2

They Know Where You Live:
Guarding Your Privacy and Identity

Cynthia Hetherington

How did they find me? That's a question many of us ask when we get unsolicited emails and spams. The answer is deceptively simple: A good deal of the information found in online databases is generated by us in our eagerness to keep our lives simple. Try the following offline example to see just how much information you generate and spread during the average day.

For 3 days, keep a journal of all the times you share your name, address, phone number, and credit card number; drive a car through a tollbooth with E-ZPass; use a grocery store coupon card; pay your bills; or answer unsolicited email. In addition, record how many credit card offers come in the mail, as well as how many telemarketing phone calls you receive. After 3 days, you'll begin to notice that you hand out your information everywhere. It is on your credit card statements as well as loans, liens, and deeds to your homes, automobiles, and other large assets. If people you do not know call your home with offers, and your shredder needs cleaning out once a week, it's time to consider minimizing your information.

After this exercise, you might think that removing yourself completely from the online world would be impossible. By paying charges with a credit card, driving quickly through tollbooths using E-ZPass, owning a home with a landline telephone, and using other day-to-day conveniences, we automatically leave an online trail.

Oddly enough, this information has always been available. It just required investigative experience and/or a serious commitment to locate these types of details through county courthouses, administrative offices, and other public record venues. But since the World Wide Web, at least 100 U.S.-based public record companies have popped up for anyone to use. These companies will locate individuals and share intimate details about where they live, who lives with them, their age, and so on—data that is available for anyone who searches for it.

Where Do Companies Get My Name?

Organizations use information from a variety of sources for a variety of reasons. You are familiar with some of them: Businesses want to send you an offer, and companies want to better understand their marketplace or to develop new products and improve customer service. In other cases, companies use information to protect you and themselves from risks related to identity fraud.

Most companies rent or buy lists of individuals who they believe are likely to be interested in certain products or services. The companies will use these lists to market to you either online or offline. The lists come from a variety of sources, including public records, telephone directories, and companies that exchange or rent their customer files for marketing purposes to other organizations that have a legitimate need for the information. The rental or exchange of customer files has been a common practice for decades and does not pose a security risk to you. The exchange usually involves only the basic contact information and very general information about your purchases. These lists are used to send mail to you, call you, email you, or text you about special promotions or offers. This enables a company to more effectively reach out to individuals who are not yet customers but who might have an interest in or need for the company's product or service.

It is also a common practice for a business or organization to create a marketing file of names, addresses, and other information related to its customers' purchases. This information may include household characteristics from surveys you fill out or from general communication with you.

However, marketing is just one use for information about you. Early detection and prevention of fraud by verifying your identity is a second use that offers significant benefits to both you and businesses. A business's ability to correctly recognize a customer, especially when transacting business over the phone, on the internet, or via a mobile device, helps reduce the chances that you will become a victim of identity fraud.

There are also other uses of personal information you may not have considered, such as courts tracing parents who fail to meet child support obligations, investigators conducting background checks for the purposes of compliance and antifraud initiatives, law enforcement agencies apprehending criminals, attorneys searching for missing heirs, and family members looking for lost relatives. These uses provide significant benefits to society as a whole and are permitted, or in some cases required, by various laws, such as requirements for background screening for child care centers and school bus drivers.

What Kind of Information Is Available?

There is a variety of information available today to businesses and organizations. Most of it is nonsensitive, but there are significant exceptions.

Public Records

Information about you may include public records, primarily from state and federal government sources: property deeds, marriage and professional licenses, and birth and death announcements.

Information is also available from court proceedings, voter registration files, driver's license records, and motor vehicle registrations. Various federal and state laws place restrictions on the use of some of these sources.

Publicly Available Information

Some information is considered to be in the public domain, which means anyone has access to it. This type of information includes telephone directory listings, professional registries, classified ads, and information posted in chat rooms, on blogs, and in sections designated as public on social networking sites.

Publicly available information is not always regulated by law, but responsible providers self-regulate its use through industry codes of conduct.

Customer Information

Customer information is collected when you provide information about yourself to an organization, whether inquiring about a product, making a donation or purchase, registering a product warranty, or receiving a service. This information includes any details you provide about how to contact you and a record of your interactions with the company or organization. This information is regulated in some cases by law and in other cases by industry practice. In addition, responsible organizations develop their own policies to ensure appropriate use of the information.

Self-Reported Information

Information you voluntarily provide on a survey or questionnaire is considered self-reported. When this type of information is collected, you should be informed of the intended uses as well as your rights and options. Both law and industry practices limit the use of this type of information.

Passively Collected Information

The internet and other technologies, including mobile devices with location-tracking features and interactive televisions, may collect information about you or your device without your having to take any action. In fact, in many cases you may not be aware that any collection is taking place. Some of this collection is necessary to provide a service, such as recording the number of times you go through the express lane of a tollbooth so you can be charged for the toll, or helping to locate your car when you need emergency assistance. Tracking features can also be used to provide relevant advertising to you, such as offering a discount on a specialty coffee from a nearby coffee shop or providing online advertising tailored to interests that have been identified based on other websites you have recently visited or keywords you have recently used in a search. Both law and industry practices limit the use of this information.

Sensitive Information

Some information, if used inappropriately, can have more serious consequences. This includes your Social Security number, driver's license number, medical records, wage and salary information, tax reports, credit report, and information that personally identifies your children.

Sensitive information should be kept confidential and is not usually provided to other organizations unless you give specific permission or unless it is permitted, or required, under state or federal law.

In order to develop credit reports, credit reporting agencies gather information from banks and other financial institutions with which you have a relationship. The Federal Trade Commission (FTC) closely regulates the use of this information as directed by the Fair Credit Reporting Act (FCRA) and the Fair and Accurate Credit Transactions Act (FACTA).

In order to assure you will be a responsible employee, tenant, or insured individual, employers, landlords, and insurance companies may ask your permission to do a background check on you. This involves verifying the information you provided on your application with the source of the data.

Background checks can also involve obtaining a credit report if your financial situation is pertinent to the employer or landlord. The FTC closely regulates uses of this information as directed by the FCRA.

How Can I Protect My Privacy?

Despite the overabundance of information shared and sold today on the web, there are a number of measures to protect your personal information. It is important to learn about these protections and how to exercise the options that are offered. Using the following tips can serve as a starting point for protecting your personal privacy.

Read the Privacy Policy

Reputable companies (such as financial institutions and credit card issuers) will tell you what information they collect and maintain, how it is being used, and when it is being shared with other parties. This is usually done in the form of a privacy policy. You can view the privacy policy of most companies on their websites or by contacting each company and asking for a copy. Companies that do not post or provide a privacy policy should be given extra scrutiny.

Act On Choices

Most companies will give you some choices regarding the use and dissemination of your personal information. Some of these choices are buried in the small print of websites or mailers, so you will have to look for them. If the company provides information about you to third parties for their marketing uses, you should be given a chance to opt out. This means you can request that the company not share information about you with third parties for marketing purposes. Look for the annual statement from your credit card company that discusses your opt-out options and act on them.

Monitor the Accuracy

Organizations should maintain appropriate procedures ensuring that the information they use about you for important or substantive decisions is accurate. You should be able to access such information if you feel it may not be accurate and have any erroneous information corrected, updated, or removed. Retrieving your credit report on a regular basis and verifying the details is a great way to monitor your private information. The following are companies that compile personal information. The vendors on this list are the market share leaders in the public records business.

Accurint, www.accurint.com

- Privacy Policy: www.accurint.com/privacy.html

- Opt-Out: Partial

- Action: www.lexisnexis.com/privacy/for-consumers/opt-out-of-lexisnexis.aspx

- Affiliation: LexisNexis

Acxiom, www.acxiom.com

- Privacy Policy: www.acxiom.com/about_us/privacy/privacy_policies/Pages/PrivacyPolicies.aspx

- Opt-Out: Yes

- Action: Email privacy@acxiom.com, or visit www.acxiom.com/about_us/privacy/consumer_ information/opt_out_request_form/Pages/Opt-OutRequestForm.aspx. (Be warned: It won't be easy to opt out without first providing more personal information.)

- Affiliation: Google, Yahoo!, Whowhere, and Lycos

Google, www.google.com

- Privacy Policy: www.google.com/intl/en/privacy.html

- Opt-Out: Partial

- Action: www.google.com/support/webmasters/ bin/answer.py?hl=en&answer=164734

InfoSpace.com, search.infospace.com/ispace/ws/index

- Privacy Policy: support.infospace.com/privacy

- Opt-Out: Yes

- Action: search.infospace.com/ispace/ws/contactUs

Intelius, www.intelius.com

- Privacy Policy: www.intelius.com/privacy.php

- Opt-Out: Yes

- Action: In order to opt out, you need to verify your identity—a faxed proof of identity is required. Proof of identity can be a state-issued ID card or driver's license. If you are faxing a copy of your driver's license, cross out the photo and the driver's license number. Intelius only needs to see the name, address, and date of birth. Fax the copy to 425-974-6194 and allow 4 to 6 weeks to process your request.

- Affiliation: AnyWho, Address.com, BackgroundCheck Gateway.com, InfoSpace.com, Peoplefinder.com,

PeopleLookup.com, Phonebook.com, ThePublicRecords.com, and ZabaSearch.

LexisNexis, www.lexisnexis.com

- Privacy Policy: www.lexisnexis.com/privacy
- Opt-Out: Partial
- Action: www.lexisnexis.com/privacy/for-consumers/opt-out-of-lexisnexis.aspx
- Affiliation: Accurint and IRBsearch

MyLife.com, www.mylife.com

- Privacy Policy: www.mylife.com/PrivacyPolicy.pub
- Opt-Out: Yes
- Action: Read the Privacy Policy section Your Choices and follow the directions.

pipl, www.pipl.com

- Privacy Policy: www.pipl.com/privacy
- Opt-Out: No
- Action: Contact MyLife Customer Care toll-free at 888-704-1900.
- Affiliation: MyLife.com

Spokeo, www.spokeo.com

- Privacy Policy: www.spokeo.com/privacy
- Opt-Out: Yes
- Action: Read the Privacy Policy section called Content Removal from Spokeo Searches.

US Search, www.ussearch.com/consumer/index.jsp

- Privacy Policy: www.ussearch.com/consumer/commerce/about/privacy.jsp?

- Opt-Out: Yes

- Action: www.ussearch.com/consumer/ala/landing.do?
  did=538

ZabaSearch, www.zabasearch.com

- Privacy Policy: www.zabasearch.com/privacy.php

- Opt-Out: Yes

- Action: www.zabasearch.com/block_records

ZoomInfo, www.zoominfo.com

- Privacy Policy: www.zoominfo.com/business/overview/
  privacy/25-privacy-policy.html

- Opt-Out: Yes

- Action: Claim your account and then remove or redact
  the details.

Obtain Credit Reports

Obtain copies of and review credit reports from the three major credit reporting agencies. To order a free annual report from one or all of the national consumer reporting companies, visit www.annualcreditreport. com, call toll-free 877-322-8228, or complete the Annual Credit Report Request Form and mail it to Annual Credit Report Request Service, P.O. Box 105281, Atlanta, GA 30348-5281. The form can be printed from ftc.gov/credit. Please note that www.annualcredit report.com is a government-recommended credit reporting service. You will be asked for personal identifiers, which might seem intrusive, but it is necessary to submit these in order to apply for your credit reports.

Keeping Your Information Offline

Once you realize there is an abundance of information on you available to even the most casual searcher, you may wish to start opting out of these company resources. There are many ways to keep your information offline:

- Have your postal mail sent to a P.O. Box and have packages delivered to your office.

- Unlist and unpublish your landline phone numbers; check with your mobile service company to find out if it sells its subscribers' information and how to opt out of that list.

- Never put your name, number, or information on any form or application without checking to see what the resale or privacy policy is.

- Mail a written request to all of your credit cards and banks requesting your personal information be removed from lists that are made available to other companies.

- Do not fill out any warranty cards; instead, save them with the original sales receipts. Providing you have both when filing a claim, the store has to honor your warranty. Otherwise, you would see "due by" dates on warranty cards.

- Do not subscribe to any magazines under your own name.

A very effective and helpful strategy is to contact your credit card companies and request to be removed from their third-party marketing lists. The lists are sent out every year, as required by law, but you may have missed the explanation in the fine print.

More tips and sites follow that will help you control, even in a small way, what is readily available to the casual searcher on the World Wide Web:

- Register with donotcall.gov to remove yourself from popular telemarketing lists.

- Stop oversharing information online in unneccessary scenarios such as social networks and blogs.

- Visit websites that follow and locate your information (e.g., ZabaSearch.), then follow the removal procedures. Some will ask you to verify your contact information, which is uncomfortable, but necessary in order to get yourself removed.

Thwarting the Cyberbully and Preventing Online Identity Theft

The attraction of reconnecting with old friends, networking with colleagues and clients, even finding long-lost loves, can now all happen in a social network from a desktop computer (or laptop, cell phone, or personal digital assistant) on a global scale. Registering requires no real effort and, most importantly, no real talent (programming skills or otherwise). With plug-and-play Web 2.0 applications (second-generation websites such as Facebook, Wikipedia, and Myspace), you simply fill in the blanks and answer a few questions, and you are able to participate in and are a part of a global network.

In the past, when websites were developed and maintained by a select few, those unique participants who loaded content onto websites controlled what "happened" on the web. Today, anyone and their grandmother can start sharing their thoughts and photos online through easily accessible social networks. And they do.

But with ease of use often comes lack of control. While people are reuniting, connecting, and sharing in the light of online social networks, the dark side is online as well. It is fomenting another world in which pedophiles are viewing the Myspace pages of children, gangs are creating Facebook profiles, and criminals are trolling for target homes to rob as owners announce vacation plans on their social networks.

Everyday Joes and Janes—millions of them—who were once content to surf the web and email their friends as their primary internet activities, are now using social tools such as Facebook and Twitter to keep everyone apprised of their day-to-day lives, often in the most minute detail.

The technology is reaching a younger demographic. Teenagers and tweens are easily and readily adapting to the technology. And to them, there is no division between their real lives and their online lives. Their physical-world lives are also their online lives, with no holding back. The younger users will say and do pretty much anything online without hesitation. On the other hand, adults and seniors are also participating in online social networks; unlike the younger set, these more mature folk, who grew up in an era of discretion and modesty, are not as open in their online social network postings. In general, younger people will join social networks openly, while adults will generally continue to use caution before sharing their lives online.

Facebook Confessions

People on Facebook have a lot of contact with one another, and those people actually care about what is said. These shifts can initially be unsettling for the first-time Facebook user. In the physical world, good or bad news would be shared over the telephone or spoken in person to a few close friends. You wouldn't stand on a mountaintop and announce to the world that you just finished a load of laundry or that you were staying home with a sick child that day. Never mind the mountaintop, you wouldn't even walk into your local grocery store and do that. Doing so would seem awkward and inappropriate. And yet, in online social networks such as Facebook or Twitter, it feels like the social norm to mention these details. In fact, it is almost a social obligation to do so.

That's where things get sticky. In an environment of such relatively uninhibited, open communication, it isn't long before overzealous opinions, little bits of rage, drunken rants, and other embarrassing entries get posted. The user could be upset, deranged, or overjoyed, and his or her natural reaction is to share the emotion—and often that sharing takes place on a social network. Friends don't let friends drive drunk, right? Be sure to take not just the keys away from that person but also the keyboard.

Sharing your thoughts and activities online in and of itself is not necessarily a problem. The problem comes when users forget that everyone in their social network is reading their posts. When you post something in frustration over your boss, co-worker, spouse, or friend, remember that the boss, co-worker, spouse, or friend—and all their networked friends (and all of *their* networked friends)—may also be reading your posts.

Want examples? Visit youropenbook.org and search the following phrases: *hate my boss*, *cheated on my husband*, or any other such confessional phrase to search public Facebook postings using Facebook's own search service.

Having second thoughts now about using Facebook? It is possible to take part in Facebook and still maintain a modicum of privacy. To accomplish this, keep the following lessons in mind:

1. *Do not write in a fury.* If you are angry, inebriated, or simply have a big secret that you are itching to share, it's time to step away from the keyboard. What you think is hysterical or outlandish to post now might only serve to embarrass you later.

2. *Do not ignore Facebook's privacy controls.* Your Facebook profile can be customized. Do it. Limit access to only your friends, friends of friends, or only yourself. Do not enter contact information, such as your phone number and address. Restrict access to your photos, birth date, religious views, and family information, among other things. Give only certain people or groups of people access to items such as photos or block specific people from seeing them.

3. *Do not post your child's name in a photo caption.* Don't use a child's name in photo tags or captions. If someone else does, delete the name's tag by clicking on Remove Tag. If your child isn't on Facebook and someone includes his or her name in a caption, ask that person to remove the name. Do not share the details of your child's life online. Soccer practice is likely on a regular schedule, which can be easily tracked by a predator reading Facebook profiles.

4. *Do not mention when you'll be away from home.* When you tell your friends through Facebook that you are not going to be home, you are inviting criminals trolling Facebook profiles—especially unsecured profiles—to your house.

5. *Do not use a weak password.* Avoid using simple names or words that can be found in a dictionary as passwords. Even with numerals tacked on the end of the word, that is not a secure password. Instead, use a knuckle-breaker password, one that requires

upper- and lower-case letters in combination with numerals and symbols. A secure password should have a minimum of eight characters.

6. *Do not put your birthday in your profile.* Your birth date is an ideal target for identity thieves who can use it to obtain more information about you, potentially gaining access to your bank or credit card accounts. If you've already entered your birth date in Facebook, go to your profile page and click on the Info tab, then on "Edit Information." Under the Basic Information section, choose to show only the month and day—or, better yet, no birth date at all.

7. *Do not let search engines find you.* To help prevent strangers from accessing your Facebook page, go to Facebook's Privacy Section and then Apps, Games and Websites. There you will see Public Search, where you have the option to enable or disable that function.

8. *Do not ignore your privacy settings.* Facebook changes its Terms of Service regularly. You must check your profile by choosing the Privacy Settings on the pull-down menu item on the right-hand side of the screen. Alternately, go to www.facebook.com/edit profile.php after you have logged in to the site. Here you will see two buttons in the upper right hand corner, View My Profile and View As. This shows you what you have available for the general public to view. Once you see how much of your page is exposed, visit the privacy settings and fine tune your profile to share only as much as you are comfortable with. To stay on top of Facebook's ever-changing privacy features, visit www.facebook.com/help/privacy often.

9. *Do not permit your children to be on Facebook.* Facebook limits its members to ages 13 and older, but children younger than 13 still use it. If you have a young child or teenager on Facebook, then become one of their online friends. It is your best chance to

provide parental oversight of what is going on in their account. Use your email address as the contact for their account so that you receive their notifications and can monitor their activities.

10. *Do not friend your employer.* Sure, it seems like a great idea to friend your boss; that is, until you decide to rant about how much you hate working overtime or you post photos of your day at the beach (um, the same day you called into work sick).

Cyberbullying, Harassment, and Stalking

What happens when the online rants and ravings in social networks are directed toward a specific individual in a cruel or demeaning fashion?

Unfortunately, these types of posts are getting more prevalent, and it's shocking how harsh and off-color some of them can be. But the real problem comes when one or more individuals start making attacks against a specific person. Some individuals post horrendous lies or attacks online against another person, with no restraint or remorse.

In the physical world, I can face off with an individual and say horrible things to him or her directly or even to others about that individual. In the physical world, this is called slander. When slanderous statements are made online in social networks or through text messages and emails, they are, by definition, stored in an electronic medium, which then turns slander into libelous action. Cyberbullying, harassment, and stalking are all libelous activity.

Whether called bullying, harassment, or stalking, the result is an attack on the person, defaming his or her name on the web. Entire websites and blogs have been devoted to defamation campaigns against an individual. These cowardly posts, written with an agenda to libel the targeted individual, are often done in anonymous fashion, making it difficult to discern the actual offender.

Attempts to locate the online poster can be made with some success. The effort requires time and expertise—two things most online users are short on, so the average victim is left with an unknown harasser. Adding insult to injury, most defamation posts do not cross the line far enough legally to merit the attention of law enforcement.

On the other hand, most victims usually have a sense of who the culprit is and might find alternatives, such as using an intermediary to stop the activity. Students are told to let teachers and administrators know if posts about themselves start appearing.

Beyond all that, there are ways to thwart and/or prevent online cyberbullying yourself. For example:

- Run your name through Google on a regular basis to monitor where your name is being mentioned online.

- Secure your online space. One way is to set your Facebook account to Private. When you allow anyone in, you are essentially giving anyone—including cyberbullies—open access to your data.

- When you do come across a cyberbully's online posting, resist the temptation to retort. Antagonizing bullies will only give them what they want: attention. If you ignore them, they will most likely move along to another (more vocal) target.

- If someone is posting inappropriate comments on a social network service, report the abusive behavior to the social network's account security (for example, by using the Report link in Facebook).

Identity Theft Online

Identity theft—the theft of your personal identifiers and their unauthorized use in fraudulent activities—predates the internet. After all, identity theft is a crime for the lazy; such thieves would rather go after the low-hanging fruit—swiping a credit card receipt off a diner's table, for example—than strain for hard-to-reach, well-protected profiles. Identity thieves are savvy enough to know that the well-protected profile is not worth pursuing.

Ironically, we fear losing our identity to theft in the online financial services we use—our credit card and bank accounts—and yet give no thought to the personal information lying open in our social network profiles. The established online financial and commerce systems are some of the most trusted sites available, using multilayered encryption software to protect our financial transactions. Of course, no one system is absolutely impenetrable, but why should a cyber thief try to steal a credit card when the internet offers up so much more easily attainable information?

Today, an identity thief need only turn to the personal profiles posted in social network sites, such as Facebook and LinkedIn, to capture key information about a targeted individual. A full name (even maiden name), date of birth, and current home location gleaned from an open social network account are sufficient data points for a thief to start creating a fraudulent profile. In fact, LinkedIn, the working professional's social network workhorse, holds a veritable goldmine of personal information for identity thieves. Consider this: LinkedIn requires its users to post schools attended and jobs held, with corresponding dates. Now layer on the personal details gleaned from linked colleagues and friends in the network, and you can rather easily crib a good list of controlled answers for most challenge questions—those security questions used to prompt for a forgotten password.

It's not impossible to lose access to your own web-based email account simply because an identity thief was able to hijack the account by answering the security challenge question after pulling the information off open source search engines, or from one or more unprotected social network profiles.

How is online identity theft prevented? In addition to the guidelines offered earlier for thwarting cyberbullying, consider the following:

- Monitor your name online. Set up a Google Alert (www.google.com/alerts) and a Tracklet (www.trackle. com) on your own name. If anything is said about you—either in a social network or elsewhere online— these services will send you a notification.

- Tweak your memorable word (in a memorable way, of course) that answers your challenge question. For example, if your first dog's name was Java, use the word *coffee* as a challenge answer and memorize that tweaked word. Or pick one obtuse word, such as *rollerblade*, to answer every challenge question and, again, memorize that obtuse word.

- If someone you haven't communicated with in ages tries to contact you in a social network, ask this user your own challenge question: "Hey, do you remember Jorge Beale getting stuck at the top of ropes in gym class?" The question can be honest or you can make one up. Pay more attention to the answer. Does it seem authentic?

- Don't publish your life story on social networks. Be discreet online; your full name and general vicinity of where you reside are sufficient identifying information. Combining information from LinkedIn with information from ZabaSearch lets a thief quickly locate your home address.

- Request to have your personal information removed from online identifying databases such as Intelius.

The internet started as a communications network among a community of mostly academics. The evolved internet technologies of today's Web 2.0 applications brought the internet to the general public: the Average Joes and Janes, who have happily become active, engaged internet users.

With the internet now open to anyone, everyone is online in some capacity. And just as there are good and not-so-good people in the physical world, there are also good and not-so-good people in the online world. With ubiquity and facility come threats and need for caution. Should you find yourself discovering the internet's dark side of identity theft, don't pack up, shut down, and remove yourself wholesale from the online world. Instead, alter or completely delete your pertinent information (i.e., date of birth, hometown name, identifying photos) from your social network profiles. The reason for editing the profile before deleting it is to let the web crawlers (Google and Bing) capture misinformation vs. accurate information. If you just shut down your account, the last information that was listed for you will be searchable for years to come.

If you use a social network infrequently—for example, as a place to view your extended family's vacation photos—then offer up only nonessential information when creating an account on the service. If you do so and use the service's provided security tools and precautions, there should be no harm to be concerned about. There should be nothing stored online that you need to be worried about, nothing for anyone to bully you for or steal from you.

Respect Web 2.0 applications. If you would not feel comfortable having your online activity broadcast through your local grocery store's public address system, while simultaneously having a giant, neon arrow pointing directly at you, then there's a good chance that your online activity has no business being online.

CHAPTER 3

Demonizing the "Other"

Eli Edwards

The objective of the online game *Border Patrol* is simple: Players keep Mexicans from crossing the United States–Mexico border at the Rio Grande "by any means necessary." It allows them to bloodily dispatch highly stereotyped Mexican characters while a tinny version of "La Cucaracha" is heard in the background. In this game, the targets are "illegal aliens" called "Mexican Nationalist," "Drug Smuggler," and "Breeder." At the end of the round, the shooter (player) receives a tally of how many "wetbacks" were killed.[1]

Computer and video gaming is a multibillion-dollar business that attracts players to websites offering Flash-based games on a variety of platforms, including sophisticated consoles such as Microsoft's Xbox and Nintendo's Wii. A player looking for a simple shoot-'em-up game is not expecting to find options filled with racist and xenophobic pro-paganda. But standard game sites such as Sangent, YouShock, Daily FreeGames.com, and Free Gaming offer these along with a range of others without any warning about the nature of their content. *Border Patrol* is also available at many extremist websites and was originally designed by and for white supremacists.[2] And such games have been around for a while. As early as 2002, the Anti-Defamation League (ADL) reported the availability of white-power–themed shoot-'em-up games such as *Ethnic Cleansing*, *Shoot the Blacks*, and *Concentration Camp Rat Hunt*.[3]

Games may be a seemingly unimportant niche of misleading content in which a minority is demonized. However, *Border Patrol* is not just an online game; it mirrors reality for some immigrants to the U.S. and reinforces the dangers they face. Real people die. In July 2008, Luis Ramirez, an undocumented Mexican immigrant, was the victim of a bias-motivated, fatal beating in Shenandoah, Pennsylvania. Originally acquitted in state court of all but minor charges in 2009, two men were convicted of the hate crime in late 2010 in federal court.[4]

As new protocols for the web come to fruition (aka Web 2.0), so-called extremist groups are exploiting them to spread lies and propaganda about people who are different based on race, religion, sexual orientation, or political affiliation.

The Colors of Misinformation: The Black Man in the White House

In the 2008 U.S. presidential election, candidate Barack Obama faced rumors that he was secretly a Muslim, despite having detailed his religious history in his memoirs. According to various rumors circulating online during that election cycle, Obama had been indoctrinated into the conservative Wahhabi (or Salafi) sect of Islam through either his Kenyan father, his Indonesian stepfather, or the Islamic madrassa school he allegedly attended in Indonesia.[5,6] Some versions further claimed that Obama's adult conversion to Christianity and his years at Trinity United Church of Christ were part of a ruse to keep his radical Muslim beliefs secret as he campaigned to become president of the U.S.[7]

Obama's election to the presidency did not put an end to the rumor; in fact, the gossip seems to have taken root and grown more popular. In a survey released in August 2010, the Pew Research Center for the People & the Press found that 18 percent of Americans believe that he is Muslim, up from 12 percent during the 2008 campaign and 11 percent after his inauguration.[8] Other statistics reveal that only one-third of Americans believe he is Christian, down from 48 percent in March 2009.

Many people point to a system of adversarial politics run amok. But there is another aspect to this rumor that will not die: the existence of what is called "hate speech" on the internet, a difficult subject to discuss. What may be "hate speech" to one person is "protected free speech" to another, which is a very subtle line. But that line is a legal one, and this discussion does not propose to draw it; but instead, it will educate internet users about sites that demonize people who are "different" from the sites' authors.

So-Called Hate Sites

What some call racism and others call hate speech has been present on the World Wide Web since its inception. One popular site, Stormfront (www.stormfront.org), bills itself as providing "White Nationalist News and Discussion for Racial Realists." Launched in 1995, it is considered the first white supremacist website.[9] As of July 2011, Stormfront had a ranking among websites accessed in the U.S. of 5,233, with more than 1,500 other websites linking to it.[10] Stormfront has always been aboveboard with its white power philosophy.[11] It has been joined by many others promoting such controversial material as racial supremacy, religious intolerance, and Holocaust denial.[12]

According to a February 2011 Simon Wiesenthal Center report on social media and digital hate speech, there are more than 14,000 digital items catalogued as racist, anti-Jewish, anti-Islamic, anti-immigrant, or terrorist speech on blogs, video sites, social networking pages, and other social media sites.[13] While these problematic sites the report describes as "devoted to hate, terrorism and extremist speech" can sometimes be obvious in their point of view, not all wear their colors so blatantly. The most famous example is www.martinlutherking.org, a Stormfront-owned website devoted to the life of the major civil rights activist (also discussed in this book's Introduction). Since the website has been the subject of much discussion since its original posting in the late 1990s, it is a good idea to read about it for yourself on sites such as Snopes.com. In this case, there are no factual inaccuracies on the site. The issues revolve around the innuendo and the links to other sites. For example, the section on recommended readings has a link to books by David Duke, a known white supremacist.

While the Stormfront site about Martin Luther King is the most famous example of this type of misleading depiction on the internet, it's not the only one. The National Socialist Movement, a neo-Nazi group, has a recruitment page for teens called Viking Youth Corps that emphasizes "honor, discipline, sound morals and loyalty," as values instilled by the organization. These are fine values, as are all the stated objectives of the organization. But if you have any blood lines from Jews or nonwhite races, don't bother applying for organization membership.[14] It is not made clear on the site why this disqualifies someone from joining.

Another example of a race-based agenda is Stormfront for Kids, a website maintained by the son of Stormfront's founder, Don Black, which encourages "white people across the globe" to "be proud of who they are."[15] Racial extremists defend use of the phrase "white pride" as being equivalent to ethnic pride and celebrating personal heritage. But the ADL has pointed out that behind the seemingly innocuous sentiment of white pride, as promoted by Black and his son, Derek, the "concept of 'victory' for whites includes the creation of ethnically cleansed living spaces."[16] ADL points out that "White Pride World Wide," a slogan that appears on the Stormfront website, involves demeaning and demonizing Jews and nonwhites. Derek Black's site Stormfront for Kids promotes other Stormfront sites. Both the ADL and the Southern Poverty Law Center have profiles of Derek Black that demonstrate his active and rising prominence in white supremacist circles.[17]

Another group dedicated to recruiting teens is called the Knights Party Youth Corp. The page that solicits members on its website has the disclaimer that the group is "only looking for white youth who are motivated by love for their race and NOT hatred for other races."[18] However, the page also notes that "white youth" should fight "for the right to be 'White and Proud!'" and fight against "racemixing."[19] The Ku Klux Klan, aka the Knights Party, which features David Duke as its first national director (formerly called a Grand Dragon), is the parent group of the Youth Corp.[20]

These are enough examples of white supremacist overtones. What's going on here is much bigger than a list of websites that demonize the "other."

Shifting to Web 2.0

"The key feature of Web 2.0 is the development of software which enables mass participation in social activities,"[21] according to Kylie Garrett, a lecturer at the Centre for Media Studies at National University of Ireland, Maynooth. The participatory aspect of Web 2.0 is perhaps its most popular feature. Instead of being passive consumers of content, people can comment on each other's content and contribute their own text, audio, and video. It is relatively easy to start and maintain a blog using software such as Blogger, LiveJournal, Movable Type, TypePad, or WordPress. YouTube hosts millions of videos from around the world. Social networking sites such as Facebook, Myspace, Xanga, and others allow people to create profiles, connect, and exchange messages with friends and find new friends and acquaintances. Twitter enables microblogging (140 characters or less) from a cell phone. These social media services, and many others, allow people to keep up with family, friends, colleagues, or other associates in synchronous and asynchronous ways, live and delayed, in chronological or thematic order, with the opportunities for others to "talk back" to the original content producer.

As Meg Smith related in Chapter 1, while social media allows us to better connect with loved ones, friends, and colleagues, these sites simultaneously make some unsavory web activities and content more easily accessible and harder to track. It has been used for numerous scams and phishing schemes, cyberbullying, and network attacks, and it is also a platform for hate or extremist speech, in ways that can make such speech anonymous, ubiquitous, more pernicious, and less accountable than ever before. And social media allow for instantaneous worldwide distribution.

Racist and Extremist Speech

So-called hate sites have long had interactive elements, especially chat rooms and forums that allow the like-minded and true believers to reinforce their messages and proselytize to new and casual website users. But the advent of social media has sparked greater interaction. In 2010, the Simon Wiesenthal Center issued "Digital Terrorism and Hate," an annual report that noted a 20-percent increase in one year in the amount of terrorist activity and hate speech found on the internet.[22] The report's list of most dangerous and offensive content includes sites such as:

- Stormfront's Twitter page

- An online game based on Chutes and Ladders released in Iran called *Snakes and Ladders*, in which the snakes include Jews, the BBC, and Obama

- Kidnapping-instruction videos posted by Hamas, the Palestinian-Islamist sociopolitical organization

- YouTube postings for anti-Jewish and anti-Christian groups in the U.S. and Russia

- The Facebook page of an anti-Christian group in Egypt[23]

Facebook has come under particular scrutiny by the Simon Wiesenthal Center, the ADL, and attorney Brian Cuban because of specific pages created by individuals and groups promoting extremist views and activities. In May 2009, Cuban pointed out a number of Holocaust denial groups and pages on Facebook, and criticized the site for deleting only some (but not all) Holocaust denial pages.[24]

In September 2010, a press release from the Simon Wiesenthal Center called attention to the more than 24 Facebook pages with the theme "Kill a Jew" created just that month.[25] In that statement, the center's associate dean, rabbi Abraham Cooper, commented:

> With the world's embrace of social networking it is not surprising that haters and those promoting terrorism increasingly focus their efforts online to denigrate their enemies as well as recruit and fundraise for their causes. That is why the Wiesenthal Center has been urging more vigilance by key internet providers during a series of briefings and meetings with officials at [Facebook], Yahoo, Google and YouTube.

Concerted efforts by so-called hate groups can exploit the ease of using social media platforms. An exacerbating factor is the relative anonymity of internet participation. The ease of creating pseudonymous and anonymous accounts gives people license to post what they might not reveal in face-to-face conversations. Racist comments posted to online newspaper sites and other popular mainstream sites are on the rise, according to the Associated Press.[26]

The Simon Wiesenthal Center asks people to report hate or terrorist sites to ireport@wiesenthal.com. The ADL has an online tool kit, "Responding to Cyberhate," that provides definitions and advice on how to deal with cyberbullying and extremist speech online.[27]

Obama and the Muslim Meme

Let's get back to the "Obama is Muslim" meme. Although this rumor was refuted multiple times on the campaign trail, it came back with a vengeance in summer 2010 and has yet to be dispelled, despite a lack of evidence. On August 27, 2010, a *Newsweek* poll discovered that many people who don't like President Obama think "it's 'definitely true' or 'probably true' that he 'sympathizes with the goals of fundamentalists who want to impose Islamic law around the world.'"[28] The *Newsweek* stories about the poll results focused on psychological factors such as "associational distortion," which describes the tendency to reinforce already negative beliefs,[29] and "motivated reasoning," which seeks information to reinforce only what a person wants to believe.[30] But with its political focus, the article glossed over how "Muslim" and "Islamic" have become slurs to inflict damage.

In summer 2010, in addition to political campaigns for the fall primary and general elections, there was a vitriolic fight over a project officially called the Park51 Center in New York City. It was dubbed the "Ground Zero Mosque" by FOX News in December 2009,[31] a fast-spreading misnomer in which some facts were blurred:

- The controversial project was never located at the former World Trade Center (aka Ground Zero), but rather two blocks away from the perimeter.

- The plan called for a community center that included a Muslim prayer space, in addition to an auditorium, theater, fitness facility, bookstore, and performing arts center. Referring to it as a "mosque" is akin to calling a YMCA a "church."

- A legitimate mosque has stood about 10 blocks away from the World Trade Center for more than 20 years.

By early summer, opposition began to grow against the project, and by August 2010, a CNN poll found that 68 percent of Americans opposed the construction of the Park51 Center.[32]

But the Park51 Center was not the only embattled project involving Islamic places of worship. A proposed mosque on Staten Island in New York City was the subject of significant debate and fear mongering, with attendees at a civic association meeting asking such questions as, "Wouldn't you agree that every terrorist, past and present, has come out of a mosque?" and "Will you denounce Hamas and Hezbollah as terrorist organizations?"[33] These arguments also played out online. Other proposed mosques in Murfreesboro, Tennessee, Sheboygan, Wisconsin, and Temecula, California, also faced protests. A *New York Times* story addressed the fear and disdain that fueled mosque opposition efforts:

> "What's different is the heat, the volume, the level of hostility," said Ihsan Bagby, associate professor of Islamic studies at the University of Kentucky. "It's one thing to oppose a mosque because traffic might increase, but it's different when you say these mosques are going to be nurturing terrorist bombers, that Islam is invading, that civilization is being undermined by Muslims." Feeding the resistance is a growing cottage industry of authors and bloggers—some of them former Muslims—who are invited to speak at rallies, sell their books and testify in churches. *Their message is that Islam is inherently violent and incompatible with America.*[34] (emphasis added)

The opposition to the Tennessee mosque went beyond rhetoric (online and off); there was a fire at the building site that damaged construction equipment. The controversy about building an Islamic cultural center so close to the former World Trade Center site was covered in newspapers and on broadcasts, but the internet allowed unedited and intentional misrepresentations of the Park51 Center story to spread quickly and unchallenged. As Mark Twain reportedly said, "A lie gets halfway around the world before the truth has a chance to get its pants on."[35]

The Park51 story was then followed by the embarrassing debacle of a fundamentalist minister in Florida, Terry Jones, who threatened to burn a copy of the Koran on the ninth anniversary of the September 11 attacks. More than 7 million results were retrieved from a Google search on the term *Pastor Terry Jones* as of July 19, 2011.[36] Jones's assertion was that "Islam promotes violence and that Muslims want to impose Sharia law in the United States."[37] As the rhetoric escalated, so did the violence. According to the Southern Poverty Law

Center, threats and violence against Muslims and Islamic houses of worship rose over the summer at the same time the Park51 Center controversy occurred.[38] This violence was not only verbal and online. In late August 2010, a New York City taxi driver was stabbed by a passenger who asked if the driver was a Muslim and then attacked the driver when he answered affirmatively.[39]

Anti-Muslim sentiment grew even as the Park51 Center and Terry Jones faded from the headlines. During the fall 2010 midterm election campaigns, anti-Muslim activists, commentators, and even prominent politicians such as former House speaker Newt Gingrich and then-Nevada senatorial candidate Sharron Angle made claims that Islamic religious law (Sharia) was encroaching upon and could overwhelm the constitutional system of the U.S.[40] One conservative media blog maintained that National Public Radio's firing of Juan Williams for remarks he made regarding Muslims and personal fears was "the latest in a series of media and political capitulations to Sharia law."[41] Angle's remarks on Sharia law trumping American jurisprudence focused particularly on Dearborn, Michigan. It does not seem coincidental that Dearborn has a population with 30 percent Arab ancestry; according to the 2000 Census, this is the highest rate of Arab-descent population in the U.S.[42,43]

Gingrich also weighed in, saying, "[w]e should have a federal law that says Sharia law cannot be recognized by any court in the United States."[44] As evidence of the need for such a law, Gingrich cited a 2009 rape case in New Jersey in which the judge discussed Sharia law when determining the requisite intent of the defendant while he was having nonconsensual sex with his wife; however, because the verdict in the case was overturned by the state appeals court, the judge's initial discussion about Sharia law had no binding effect, which renders Gingrich's point moot.[45] Amid the growing backlash of anti-Muslim rhetoric and sentiment, the state of Oklahoma passed a ballot measure in fall 2010, approved by nearly 70 percent of voters, that prohibits judges from making decisions that are based on or drawn from foreign precedents.[46] On November 8, 2010, a federal judge temporarily blocked implementation of the ballot measure in response to a lawsuit brought by the Oklahoma executive director of the Council on American-Islamic Relations.[47] In his complaint, Muneer Awad argued that the measure condemned his faith. Thus it violated his

First Amendment rights, and it invalidated his will, which was based in part on Sharia.[48]

Sadly, the "Obama is Muslim" rumors (which continued into 2011) are not simply political pranks in a fraught presidential election year. They are a symptom of how the demonizing of people who look or seem different from "us" has taken hold on the internet and through social media, making it increasingly difficult to address and debunk rumors outright. According to Mark Weitzman of the Simon Wiesenthal Center, the recession and continuing joblessness, along with the election of the first African-American president in the U.S. "has made for a more vocal hate community. This is an unprecedented time in American history and a dangerous time because of the combination of factors."[49]

Extremist groups can seize opportunities made readily available by social media to spread their hate, making their insults, lies, and threats well-known in the digital slipstream of online communication and entertainment. Misinformation that plays on racial, ethnic, religious, gender, and sexual fears is found within numerous tweets, Facebook walls, blogs, and news story comments, among other messages. Weitzman urges educators to "guide students toward proper web tools." But critical awareness of this type of intentional misinformation by teachers and schoolchildren should not be the only response.

The First Amendment to the U.S. Constitution supports free speech, and (rightly or wrongly) the judicial system has historically been reluctant to rein in all but the most egregious examples of extremist speech. Unlike certain European countries that prohibit specific hate speech, the U.S. protects speech that is insulting, discriminatory, and divisive, whether obliquely or subtly, with blatant falsehoods or shaded inferences. But the counterbalance is to confront pernicious, misleading, or hateful speech directly rather than censoring it. Supreme Court justice Louis D. Brandeis wrote, "If there be time to expose through discussion the falsehood and fallacies, to avert the evil by the processes of education, the remedy to be applied is more speech, not enforced silence."[50] The demonization of people who are "different" on the kinds of sites described in this chapter is a challenge to thoughtful citizens who respect the rights protected under that amendment. Professor Stephen Newman of York University elaborated on the importance of addressing extremist speech and prejudicial misrepresentation:

> Our faith in democracy rests on the belief that most if not quite all of our fellow citizens share our commitment to democratic values and are sufficiently rational to weigh the opinions to which they are exposed in light of their political and normative commitments. It is only for this reason that we have the confidence to fight words with words, believing that we can defeat evil ideas by exposing them for what they are.[51]

To be responsible citizens in a functional, open, and productive democracy, we need to refuse and reject messages that demonize others. Content that plays to prejudices and discriminatory attitudes must be challenged with skepticism, critical thinking, and a willingness to stand up for the truth.

Resources for Teaching Tolerance

In addition to Appendix A: "Evaluating Websites," these materials from credible organizations are available to teach respect for people of all races, religions, nationalities, and sexual orientations.

Climate of Fear: Latino Immigrants in Suffolk County, N.Y., Southern Poverty Law Center, September 2009, accessed May 23, 2011, www.splcenter.org/sites/default/files/downloads/splc_suffolk_report_0.pdf.

Law Enforcement Agency Resource Network, Anti-Defamation League, accessed May 23, 2011, www.adl.org/learn/default.htm.

Karen F. Balkin, ed., *Extremist Groups: Opposing Viewpoints,* Farmington Hills, MI: Greenhaven Press, 2005.

The Nativist Lobby: Three Faces of Intolerance, Southern Poverty Law Center, February 2009, accessed May 23, 2011, www.splcenter.org/sites/default/files/downloads/splc_nativist lobby.pdf.

The Second Wave: Return of the Militias, Southern Poverty Law Center, August 2009, accessed May 23, 2011, www.splcenter. org/sites/default/files/downloads/The_Second_Wave.pdf.

Simon Wiesenthal Center, Digital Terrorism and Hate: Interactive Report on the Internet (annual), first edition 1998, on CD-ROM.

Ten Ways to Fight Hate: A Community Response Guide, Southern Poverty Law Center, 2010, accessed May 23, 2011, www.splcenter.org/sites/default/files/downloads/publication/ Ten_Ways_2010.pdf.

Endnotes

1. See the game *Border Patrol* at nerdnirvana.org/g4m3s/borderpatrol.htm, accessed May 23, 2011.

2. A search on Google with the terms *border*, *patrol*, and *game* brings up a results page in which one of the top results is the extremist website Resist, which is run by white supremacist Tom Metzger, the founder of White Aryan Resistance. See www.google.com/search?hl=&q=border+patrol+game&sourceid=navclient ff&rlz=1B3GGGL_enUS283US284&ie=UTF-8, accessed May 23, 2011.

3. Julia Scheeres, "Games Elevate Hate to Next Level," *Wired,* February 20, 2002, accessed May 23, 2011, www.wired.com/culture/lifestyle/news/2002/02/50523 #ixzz140qqy87c.

4. *USA v. Brandon Piekarsky and Derrick Donchak* filed in United States District Court for the Middle District of Pennsylvania in Scranton on December 10, 2009.

5. *Wahhabi* is defined by Merriam-Webster as "a puritanical Muslim sect founded in Arabia in the eighteenth century."

6. In January 2007, then-senator Obama's staff issued a press release to debunk claims by the *Washington Times* and Fox News that the senator attended a madrassa school in Indonesia.

7. For one such deconstructed tale, see David Corn, "O'Donnell Aide: Obama Is a Secret Muslim," Mother Jones, September 20, 2010, accessed May 23, 2011, motherjones.com/politics/2010/09/odonnell-aide-obama-is-secret-muslim.

8. "Growing Number of Americans Say Obama Is a Muslim," Pew Research Center, August 19, 2010, accessed May 23, 2011, pewresearch.org/pubs/1701/poll-obama-muslim-christian-church-out-of-politics-political-leaders-religious.

9. Anti-Defamation League, "Hate on the World Wide Web: A Brief Guide to Cyberspace Bigotry," October 1998, accessed May 23, 2011, www.adl.org/special_reports/hate_on_www/print.asp.

10. Ranking confirmed on Alexa's "Stormfront.org Site Info" page on July 19, 2011, www.alexa.com/siteinfo/stormfront.org.

11. Alexa also tracks website reviews—Stormfront has 40 5-star reviews compared with 13 1-star reviews. All of the reviews acknowledge the white national theme of the site, but some claim that it is "leftist" opponents of the site who are hate-filled and vitriolic. At least two 5-stars reviewers claim to be nonwhite.

12. Anti-Defamation League, "Hate on the World Wide Web."

13. Simon Wiesenthal Center, "2011 Digital Terrorism & Hate Report Launched at Museum of Tolerance New York," News Releases for 2011, accessed July 19, 2011, www.wiesenthal.com/site/apps/nlnet/content2.aspx?c=lsKWLbPJLnF&b=6478433&ct=9141065.

14. Viking Youth Corp., "What a Viking Youth Is," accessed May 23, 2011, www.nsm88.org/youth/vycjoin.html.

15. Derek Black, "Stormfront for Kids," accessed May 23, 2011, www.stormfront.org/kids.

16. Anti-Defamation League, "Extremism in America—Don Black/Stormfront," accessed May 23, 2011, www.adl.org/learn/ext_us/Don-Black/default.asp?LEARN_Cat=Extremism&LEARN_SubCat=Extremism_in_America&xpicked=2&item=DBlack.

17. Southern Poverty Law Center, "Derek Black," Intelligence Files, accessed May 23, 2011, www.splcenter.org/get-informed/intelligence-files/profiles/derek-black.

18. The Knights Party Youth Corp, accessed May 23, 2011, kkk.bz/main/?page_id=381.

19. Ibid.

20. "What Is 33/6," The Knights Party, accessed July 19, 2011, www.kkk.bz/what_is_33.htm.

21. Kylie Jarrett, "Interactivity Is Evil! A Critical Investigation of Web 2.0," *First Monday*, 13 (March 2008) 3-3, accessed May 23, 2011, firstmonday.org/htbin/cgiwrap/bin/ojs/index.php/fm/article/view/2140/1947.

22. "Terrorists Targeting Children Via Facebook, Twitter," FOXNews.com, March 15, 2010, accessed May 23, 2011, www.foxnews.com/scitech/2010/03/15/terrorists-targeting-children-via-facebook-twitter.

23. "World Wide Web of Hate," FOXNews.com, March 15, 2010, accessed May 23, 2011, www.foxnews.com/slideshow/scitech/2010/03/15/world-wide-web-hate#slide=1.

24. Ki Mae Heussner, "Facebook Under Fire for Allowing Holocaust Deniers," ABC News, May 12, 2009, accessed May 23, 2011, abcnews.go.com/Technology/AheadoftheCurve/story?id=7566812&page=1. See also Brian Cuban, "Open Letter to Facebook CEO Zuckerberg," The Cuban Revolution, May 10, 2009, accessed May 23, 2011, www.briancuban.com/open-letter-to-facebook-ceo-mark-zuckerberg.

25. Simon Wiesenthal Center, "'Kill A Jew Day': Wiesenthal Center Identifies Spike in Virulent Anti-Jewish Facebook Pages," September 27, 2010, accessed May 23, 2011, www.wiesenthal.com/site/apps/nlnet/content2.aspx?c=lsKWLb PJLnF&b=4441467&ct=8716279.

26. Jesse Washington, "Racist Messages Pose Quandary for Mainstream Sites," *Seattle Times,* September 25, 2010, accessed July 19, 2011, seattletimes.nw source.com/html/nationworld/2012995082_apusonlineracism.html.

27. Anti-Defamation League, "Responding to Cyberhate: Toolkit for Action," August 2010, accessed May 23, 2011, www.adl.org/internet/Binder_final.pdf.

28. Jonathan Alter, "How Obama Can Fight the Lies," *Newsweek,* August 28, 2010, accessed May 23, 2011, www.newsweek.com/2010/08/28/alter-how-obama-can-fight-the-lies.html.

29. Sharon Begley quotes Alter, defining associational distortion (as applied to Obama) as the phenomenon of "[M]ore and more voters don't like him personally and so are increasingly ready to believe anything critical (and to them, being Muslim is a negative) about someone they are already inclined to resent." Sharon Begley, "Why the Belief That Obama Is Muslim?" *Newsweek*, August 31, 2010, accessed May 23, 2011, www.newsweek.com/2010/08/31/why-the-belief-that-obama-is-muslim.html.

30. Motivated reasoning, as defined in the article, is "[Seeking] out information that confirms what they already believe ... [users don't] search rationally for information that either confirms or disconfirms a particular belief." Ibid.

31. "Controversy Surrounds Ground Zero Mosque/Cultural Center," *The O'Reilly Factor*, FOX News, December 21, 2009.

32. Thomas Rhiel, "Poll: 68% of Americans Oppose 'Ground Zero Mosque'," *Talking Points Memo,* August 11, 2010, accessed May 23, 2011, tpmlivewire. talkingpointsmemo.com/2010/08/poll-68-of-americans-oppose-ground-zero-mosque.php.

33. Paul Vitello, "Heated Opposition to a Proposed Mosque," *New York Times*, June 10, 2010, accessed May 23, 2011, www.nytimes.com/2010/06/11/nyregion/11mosque.html.

34. Laurie Goodstein, "Across Nation, Mosque Projects Meet Opposition," *New York Times*, August 7, 2010, accessed May 23, 2011, www.nytimes.com/2010/08/08/us/08mosque.html.

35. This statement is attributed to others as well, with variations.

36. Google search on *Terry Jones Pastor* from July 19, 2011. Jones did burn a Koran in March of 2011, which led to violent protest in Afghanistan and the death of 20 people, including 11 at a United Nations protest. Matt Gutman, Nick Schifrin, Agha Aleem, and Lee Ferran, "Pastor Terry Jones Receives Death Threats After Koran Burning," ABC News, April 4, 2011, accessed July 19, 2011, abcnews.go.com/US/pastor-terry-jones-receives-deaths-koran-burning/story?id=13289242.

37. Russell Goldman, "Who Is Terry Jones? Pastor Behind 'Burn a Koran Day'," September 7, 2010, accessed May 23, 2011, abcnews.go.com/US/terry-jones-pastor-burn-koran-day/story?id=11575665.

38. Heidi Beirich, "Wave of Hate Crimes Directed at Muslims Breaks Out," Hatewatch, Southern Poverty Law Center, August 26, 2010, accessed May 23, 2011, www.splcenter.org/blog/2010/08/26/wave-of-hate-crimes-directed-at-muslims-breaks-out/#more-4680.

39. Aaron Katersky, Mark Crudelle, and Richard Esposito, "'Are You Muslim?' Question Leads to Cabbie Stabbing, Hate Crime Charge," The Blotter, ABC News, August 25, 2010, accessed May 23, 2011, abcnews.go.com/Blotter/muslim-question-leads-cabbie-stabbing-hate-crime-charge/story?id=11480081.

40. Brian Montopoli, "Fears of Sharia Law in America Grow Among Conservatives," Political Hotsheet, CBS News, October 13, 2010, accessed May 23, 2011, www.cbsnews.com/8301-503544_162-20019405-503544.html.

41. Brigitte Gabriel and Guy Rodgers, "NPR, Juan Williams, and Sharia Law," Human Events, November 7, 2010, accessed May 23, 2011, www.humanevents.com/article.php?id=39797.

42. Greg Sargent, "Sharron Angle on Sharia Law in America: 'That's What I Had Read'," Plum Line, *Washington Post*, October 13, 2010, accessed May 23, 2011, voices.washingtonpost.com/plum-line/2010/10/sharron_angle_on_sharia_law_in.html.

43. U.S. Census Bureau, DP-2. "Profile of Selected Social Characteristics: 2000," accessed May 23, 2011, factfinder.census.gov/servlet/QTTable?_bm=y&-geo_id=16000US2621000&-qr_name=DEC_2000_SF3_U_DP2&-ds_name=DEC_2000_SF3_U&-_lang=en&-redoLog=false&-_sse=on.

44. Montopoli, "Fears of Sharia Law."

45. Ibid.

46. Andy Barr, "Oklahoma Bans Sharia Law," Politico, November 3, 2010, accessed May 23, 2011, www.politico.com/news/stories/1110/44630.html.

47. Tim Talley, "Court Blocks Okla. Amendment on Islamic Law," Associated Press, November 8, 2010, accessed May 23, 2011, www.katu.com/news/national/106915703.html?ref=morestories.

48. Ibid.

49. Imaeyen Ibanga, "Hate Groups Effectively Use Web as a Recruiting Tool," ABC News, June 12, 2009, accessed May 23, 2011, abcnews.go.com/print?id=7822417.

50. *Whitney v. California*, 274 US 357, 377 (1927).

51. Stephen Newman, "Should Hate Speech Be Allowed on the Internet?: A Reply to Raphael Cohen-Almagor," *Amsterdam Law Forum,* 2010, 122, accessed May 23, 2011, ojs.ubvu.vu.nl/alf/rt/printerFriendly/121/225.

CHAPTER 4

Ebuyer Beware

Ben Fractenberg

Most people think they could never fall for an online scam or have their identity stolen as they are conducting business online. They are wrong. In April 2010, while reporting for a Manhattan news site, a friend sent me a text saying that my email may have been hacked. Sure enough, my account was sending everyone in my address book emails with links to various products, including Viagra. The messages went to everyone: friends, family, and even business contacts. Luckily, I was able to regain control of my account by changing the password. But for days afterward, I wondered where else I needed to bolster my online security.

I'm still not sure how my account was hacked: Perhaps I clicked on a link I shouldn't have, or a vendor from whom I purchased something online may have been hacked, or maybe it was related to a security breach with my email provider. In any case, today I am more vigilant about the emails I open, and I make sure to change my password every few months.

Here's another popular scam with multiple versions appearing in our mailboxes regularly: You get a strange message. The person identifies himself as your friend and says he is in London and was mugged the night before. His flight home is leaving in a couple of hours, and he has no way to pay the hotel bill. They won't let him leave. The friend then asks if you could wire him money to pay for the hotel and get him to the airport.

Become suspicious quickly. If your friend had been mugged and left without money or identification, local authorities would be involved. It seems obvious to many that this is a scam, but it is still very popular and a lot of people still fall for it.

Maxing You Out

In 2008, hackers used spyware to steal credit card information from a payment processor handling about 100 million credit card transactions each month.[1] The company, Heartland Payment Systems, reported that the spyware stole information including names, credit and debit card numbers, and expiration dates.[2]

Credit card fraud costs the U.S. card payment industry about $8.6 billion annually, with the bulk of losses hitting card users, according to Boston-based research firm Aite Group, LLC.[3]

Stealing credit information over the internet or via phone accounts for 10 percent of all money lost in credit card fraud.[4] This can happen when an unsuspecting person gives personal information to a fake telemarketer or tries to purchase an item through a bogus website.

And, unfortunately, your information is never completely safe, no matter how secure you think a company's card-processing system is. Many reliable companies use third-party payment processing centers that consumers know very little about.

Using a credit card to purchase goods and services online is still the safest way to go. Transactions can be disputed, and federal law limits your liability to $50 if you report any unauthorized charges within 60 days of receiving your statement.[5] But it is important to check your account regularly to see if any questionable transactions appear on your statement.

On the merchant's end, it is difficult to always verify that the person using a credit card is the owner of that card.

In another credit scam, people receive an email stating that their bank, credit card, or email account is going to expire unless they fill in personal information, generally including Social Security numbers, as well as check routing numbers and bank account numbers.

No legitimate website would ever ask you to send such sensitive information via email. You should be immediately suspicious of any email that requests personal or financial information.

If you have any questions about using your credit cards online, or if you believe your information may have been compromised, call the Federal Trade Commission's ID Theft Clearinghouse at 877-438-4338 (toll free), or visit its website at www.consumer.gov/idtheft.

Some New Ways Scammers Are Looking to Liberate Your Money

With new communication, networking, and financial transaction tools come new ways to rip you off and steal your identity.

What new scams are out there? How do we protect ourselves?

There are about 500 million people with Facebook accounts; according to the site, users are spending a combined 700 billion minutes per month networking. All of these people are navigating an ever-changing world of new applications and features.

One of the most effective ways for scammers to steal your account is through so-called phishing schemes. Phishing is a process used to steal personal information such as usernames and passwords by getting people to fill out fraudulent forms or send them in response to spam emails. The intent isn't the mere fun of stealing your identity; it's so the scammers can steal your money.

An easy way for hackers to fool people is by creating a fake Facebook landing page. For example, they create a link to an application, and then create a page that looks exactly like a Facebook page. Once you click on that link, you're asked to enter your login information. And that's all someone needs to access your account.

The best way to tell if a landing page is authentic is through the URL. A fake page might have the word *Facebook* in the address, but it will also likely include some kind of extension (e.g., www.facebook. fungames.com).

If you are not sure about the validity of the login, simply type the www.facebook.com URL into your browser to take you to the authentic Facebook login page.

Another popular trick is creating applications that dupe people into spending money on services they don't want. Many of the apps masquerade as quizzes that request personal information to complete the test. If you use Facebook long enough, you're sure to run into them.

One test appeared as an ad for a "10 Minute Mind Quiz," but it is fortunately no longer live.[6] By clicking on the ad, you were rerouted to a site where you were asked 10 easy questions. At the end of the test, you were asked to enter your cell phone number so the results could be texted to you.

But along with your score is a monthly charge on your cell phone bill. According to the fine print below the application: "This content will cost from $9.99 to $14.99 per month and will be sent to your cell."

Unfortunately, many people don't read the fine print. What they assumed would be only a 10- or 20-cent text message charge actually ended up costing the equivalent of several long distance calls a month.

A particularly pernicious bug that has been around for a number of years is the Koobface worm (also discussed in Chapter 1). While it may be viewed as a danger of social media, it is simultaneously a business scheme that results in big profits for the criminals behind it. Koobface, which is an anagram for *Facebook*, targets Microsoft Windows users who have both Facebook and Myspace accounts.

The worm sends users a message supposedly from one of their contacts, asking them to check out a video. When users click on the link, they are requested to upgrade their Flash player in order for the clip to play. Doing so may or may not provide the video or Flash upgrade, but it will definitely give you the Koobface worm, which will then log in to your account and start sending messages to your contacts.

Once the virus is on your computer, it can gather sensitive financial information, including credit card and Social Security numbers gleaned from online purchases or login information from sites like craigslist or Amazon.com.

Craigslist is the 36th-busiest site in the world and sixth in the U.S. in terms of page views, as ranked by Alexa.com.[7] The network for classified ads and forums covers more than 500 cities in 50 different countries, according to the Pew Internet & American Life Project. The site also generates 50 million new classified ads each month.[8]

The country's most popular classified site is also one of the most popular for electronic fraud. One typical situation involves vulnerable 20-somethings trying to find affordable housing in large cities such as New York. For example, an ad seems ideal for a one-bedroom apartment in the heart of Greenwich Village that allows pets and costs about $1,200 a month. Once the potential tenant responds to the ad, someone who sounds legitimate sends a reply, saying that he owns the apartment and is away for an extended period on business. He doesn't have time to fly back to the U.S., so instead, he deals with subtenants online and has a friend look after the place. This is all plausible in our plugged-in society.

The owner says that in order to get the place, the potential renter can simply wire him a deposit and the first month's rent. After he receives the funds, he will send the key to the potential renter.

See this scam for what it is. Don't let the temptation of a great deal cloud your judgment.

Wire-money scams are among the most popular varieties on craigslist. They typically take the same form: Someone who lives far away wants you to send them money in return for goods or services.

Another popular craigslist scam involves phishing for people's account information through a fake eBay site. Imagine browsing craigslist looking for a new camera and seeing an ad for a specific model that is in the right price range. You reply to the ad, and you receive a link to what looks like the same product on eBay. You are then asked to enter your eBay login information to bid on the item.

However, the site is a fake, and you've just given your login information to someone who can now use it to sell other bogus goods from your account.

As with the Facebook phishing scam, your best protection is knowing when a site is an imitation; be sure to stick with your gut feelings if a deal seems too good to be true.

Other craigslist scams include emails claiming to be from the site and offering to "guarantee your transaction." According to craigslist, the site never guarantees transactions; it is merely a platform and not directly involved in any transactions.

Money Laundering

In September 2010, the U.S. government charged dozens of people with conspiracy to commit bank fraud by using computer worms and viruses to steal password information and drain more than $3 million from U.S. bank accounts. The focus in *USA v. Svechinskaya et al.*[9] was on the use of "mules," or people who are recruited to open bank accounts under false names and transfer the funds obtained by the theft into accounts in eastern Europe. This is big business and hard to pinpoint because of the international nature of the schemes. The investigation, known as "Zeus Trojan," might lead to an international cybercrime group that allegedly stole almost $10 million from U.K. accounts. Worms and viruses that drain bank accounts from major financial institutions such as JPMorgan Chase & Co. and PNC Financial Services are examples of intentional misinformation, this time in the form of computer code. The customer whose account has been robbed is the ultimate victim.

In 2009, the Metropolitan Police in London shut down more than 1,200 websites that advertised the sale of popular merchandise, such as UGG boots and Tiffany jewelry, and then shipped counterfeits, or nothing, to the shoppers who purchased these goods using credit cards. The risk is not just financial; it also involves the possibility of identity theft. These sites were supposedly run from Asia, according to the Central e-Crime Unit, even though the domain names ended in the "co.uk" suffix that British companies use when registering their sites.[10]

By December 2010, 77 percent of Americans were using the internet, according to a study by the Pew Internet & American Life Project.[11] That same year there were 303,809 complaints of internet fraud, according to the Internet Crime Complaint Center (IC3).[12] This was the second-highest amount in the organization's 10 years of tracking online fraud.

New scams are launched regularly to try and dupe us out of our money. We are familiar with many of them, such as the infamous Nigerian Letter, which is discussed later in this chapter. But many more sophisticated scams have been hatched. It is our responsibility to educate ourselves about what forms they may take. The Nigerian Letter has actually morphed into a more sophisticated money laundering scheme that has resulted in American citizens serving jail time.

Bogus Job Ads

According to the British voluntary nonprofit site Money Laundering and Reshipping Fraud (www.bobbear.co.uk), there has been an enormous increase in bogus job ads. Criminals send unsolicited emails or advertise bogus job opportunities on legitimate internet employment sites to recruit "money transfer agents" with bank or PayPal accounts. They offer home-based employment as an agent who receives fake checks or stolen money transfers as payment, sometimes for products that the company claims to supply. Then the payment is passed on to the company via a money transfer company, such as Western Union, minus a commission for the agent. The ultimate destination of the funds is usually an organized crime syndicate outside the U.S., which makes finding the primary criminals unlikely, even when their U.S. collaborators are caught and prosecuted.

Another phony job scam is the solicitation of "newspaper job advertisement placers," where the potential mark is assigned to place job ads in local newspapers in return for a specific sum of money for each one. None of these jobs exist; the criminals cannot place these ads themselves or are unwilling to risk placing them.

A variation of this fraud involves reshipping agents: the people who accept packages at their home addresses and forward them on to the criminals who hired them. This type of fraud, well documented by the U.S. Postal Service, leaves the unsuspecting agent as the only contactable "fall guy," who is guilty of a federal crime for handling stolen goods. The victims are sometimes referred to as "reshipping donkeys."

Another variation involves purchase agents who are offered bogus jobs. One of their first tasks is to purchase equipment for the company on a personal credit card, all paid for by funds that the scammers directly transfer into this account. There are two variants on this theme. In one, the victim gives the criminals his or her credit card account information so funds can supposedly be transferred into the victim's personal account. The other variant is a nonexistent job as a "personal shopper" who purchases goods with his or her own credit card and has the goods shipped directly to overseas addresses. In order to make these schemes happen, victims have to give the criminals their credit card information and home addresses. The transferred funds eventually turn out to be fraudulent, which also wrecks the victims' credit worthiness in the future. Many of these schemes originate in eastern Europe or Russia.

No legitimate company would offer these jobs to a home-based private individual. The originating companies are most likely criminal fronts that have been created to fence stolen goods or defraud individuals. They sometimes give an air of legitimacy by displaying bogus VeriSign logos and other certificates. To protect yourself, make sure

that the URL of the pop-up seal verification page begins with the
address https://seal.verisign.com.

The Money Laundering and Reshipping Fraud site also lists
dozens of companies that are suspected of engaging in this type of
activity. Check it out before you buy.

Esellers Beware

Buyers aren't the only ones who need to beware; sellers are also fre-
quent targets for fraud. One popular scheme is for a scammer to
answer an ad and then meet the seller, offering to pay for the item
with what looks like a cashier's check. Often scammers will even
present a check for more than the item's listed price, saying they trust
the seller to wire them the difference. After the seller cashes the
check, it often takes the bank several days to determine it is a forgery.
By then, the scammers are long gone, along with the merchandise.

According to craigslist, most scams involve one or more of the
following:

- Inquiry from someone far away, often in another
  country

- Western Union, MoneyGram, cashier's check, money
  order, shipping service, escrow service, or a
  "guarantee"

- Inability or refusal to meet face-to-face before
  consummating a transaction

Craigslist advises users to deal only with local people they can
meet in person. According to the site, "you will avoid 99 percent of
the scam attempts [by doing this]."

Another scam involved with receiving money was the Economic
Stimulus Scam, which was popular during 2009 according to the
Internet Crime Report. Victims reported receiving a recorded telephone message from someone who sounded like President Obama.
The recording advised them they could apply for government funding
from the stimulus package by visiting www.nevergiveitback.com or
www.myfedmoney.com.

Victims were then asked to enter personal information and were
directed to a page informing them of their eligibility. They were

required to pay a $28 application fee to receive the funds, which never came, of course.

There are so many new scams being invented that it's impossible to keep track of them all. However, by following some simple, commonsense rules, you should be able to avoid falling for any of them. Always verify a website's authenticity before entering personal information. Never wire money to someone you don't know, especially in another country. Never download a file unless you are absolutely certain it's from a legitimate site.

Going, Going, Gone: Online Auctions

Online auction fraud, which generally refers to scams involving the misrepresentation of items sold or the nondelivery of items purchased through online auctions, accounted for slightly more than 10 percent of all complaints made in 2010, according to the IC3.[13]

Though most auction sites are legitimate, scammers often use them to dupe trusting buyers. For example, a buyer might go to a site such as eBay in hopes of buying a high-ticket item like a computer. When the buyer makes a bid, the seller replies directly, accepting the offer and asking the buyer to wire the money.

As you may have already guessed, the computer never arrives.

Another popular fraud involves scammers offering losing bidders of legitimate auction sites a "second chance" to buy the item(s) they wanted at a reduced price. They too ask the buyer to wire them money and then disappear.

As on craigslist, scammers will also target auction sellers by making the winning bid and then offering to pay with a phony cashier's check. Again, in an effort to entice the potential buyer, they will often make the check out for a price that's higher than they agreed, saying the seller can just wire them the difference.

Fraudulent scams extend the world over. Although vampires may be the first image to pop into your mind when you think of Romania, internet auction fraud is actually the most prevalent crime associated with that country, according to the IC3.[14] Romanian-based scammers will often pose as U.S. citizens on popular auction sites. Buyers presenting bids are told to wire money via Western Union to a business partner in a European country. A more recent trend is to ask a buyer to make a bank-to-bank wire transfer, which goes through American banks before being routed to Bucharest, Romania, or Riga, Latvia. Once the money is wired, there is little recourse for the fraud victim. Because the fraud is being initiated overseas, it is very difficult for U.S. authorities to prosecute the scammers.

More Frog Than Prince: The Nigerian Letter

If you've had an email account for a few years, you've probably received at least one message from someone claiming to be a Nigerian official, a businessman, or even a prince who urgently needs to wire millions of dollars out of the country.

The message will generally go into detail about complex international business rules and political strife in the African country, which requires someone abroad to receive the payment. For your help with this transaction, you will get a small percentage of the financial largess.

Of course, once someone agrees to help with the transaction, problems start to arise. Officials need to be bribed. A "deposit" needs to be made into a Nigerian account before you receive the funds. Just when the victims think they are finally going to see the money, something else inevitably arises. When a victim finally wises up, the perpetrators may still try to drain his or her bank account by using personal information they have gathered in order to steal the victim's identity.

While most of us are familiar with this scam and find it obviously phony, enough victims fall prey each year to generate millions of dollars.

According to the Federal Bureau of Investigation (FBI), some victims have even traveled to Nigeria where they have been imprisoned for violating Section 419 of the Nigerian Criminal Code for attempting to illegally divert funds out of the country.[15] Because of this law, the scam is sometimes referred to as "419 Fraud."

The following is an example letter from Fight Identity Theft:

Dear Sir,

Urgent and confidential business proposal

I am Mariam Abacha, widow of the late Nigerian head of state, Gen. Sani Abacha. After the death of my husband who died mysteriously as a result of cardiac arrest, I was informed by our lawyer, Bello Gambari, that my husband who at that time was the president of Nigeria called him and conducted him round his apartment and showed him four metal boxes containing money all in foreign exchange and he equally made him believe that those boxes are for onward transfer to his overseas counterpart for personal investment.

Along the line, my husband died and since then the Nigerian government has been after us, molesting, policing and freezing our bank accounts and even my eldest son right now is in detention. My family account in Switzerland worth US$22,000,000.00 and 120,000,000.00 Dutch Mark has been confiscated by the government. The government is interrogating him (my son Mohammed) about our asset and some vital documents. It was in the course of these, after the burial rite and customs, that our lawyer saw your name and address from the publication of the Nigerian business promotion agency. This is why I am using this opportunity to solicit for your co-operation and assistance to help me as a very sincere responsible person. I have all the trust in you and I know that you will not sit on this money.

I have succeeded in carrying the four metal boxes out of the country, with the aid of some top government official, who still show sympathy to my family, to a neighboring country (Accra-Ghana) to be precise. I pray you would help us in getting this money transferred over to your country. Each of these metal boxes contains US$5,000,000.00 (five million United States dollars only) and together these four boxes contain US20,000,000.00 (twenty million United States dollars only). This is actually what we have moved to Ghana.

Therefore, I need an urgent help from you as a man of God to help get this money in Accra-Ghana to your country. This money, after getting to your country, would be shared according to the percentage agreed by both of us. Please note that this matter is strictly confidential as the government which my last husband was part of is still under surveillance to probe us.

You can contact me through my family lawyer as indicated above and also to liaise with him toward the effective completion of this transaction on tel/fax No xxx-x-xxxxxx as he has the mandate of the family to handle this transaction.

Thanks and best regard,
Mrs. Mariam Abacha[16]

The Nigerian Letter scam has actually been around since the 1920s at least, when it was known as the Spanish Prisoner Con. The first incarnation targeted wealthy businessmen in a letter sent via snail mail, enlisting help in smuggling the son of a wealthy family out of a Spanish prison. The letter promised that the family would provide a handsome reward for helping to free their son, but, of course, the businessman would first have to pay a small sum to release the young man.

The scam letter morphed into its modern form and settled into its headquarters in Lagos, Nigeria, where highly organized gangs run the scam. Though the letter is most closely associated with Nigeria, it can also originate from Sierra Leone or the Ivory Coast, and sometimes from European nations such as Spain.

The FBI asks that you never directly reply to an email asking for your personal financial information. Remember, in many cases, these are dangerous criminals who are using the scam to fund other illicit activity like drug trafficking and credit card fraud. Instead, send the letter to the U.S. Secret Service Financial Crimes Division (www.secretservice.gov/criminal.shtml), your local FBI office (www.fbi.gov/contact-us/field), or the U.S. Postal Inspection Service (postalinspectors.uspis.gov). All of these URLs contain a .gov domain, assuring that you are dealing with a real government agency.

Unfortunately, there is only so much that American agencies can do since the perpetrators are almost always out of U.S. jurisdiction. The best way to fight the Nigerian Letter is through raising awareness to prevent others from falling victim to the scam.

The Nigerian Letter on Steroids

In early 2008, a woman in Washington State was sentenced to 2 years in prison for conspiracy to commit bank, wire, and mail fraud.[17] Her crime? Intentionally aiding criminals in Lagos, Nigeria, in carrying out a scam. She had contacted unwary victims in the U.S. who were willing to cash checks. After depositing the checks, they were told to take commissions for their participation and wire the difference to the scammers or to people, including this woman, who acted as their agent. Only after they wired the money did the victims find out the checks were counterfeit and that they had been defrauded. In this particular case, the woman had been sent the names of potential victims, along with fake blank checks from major businesses. She was supposed to fill in the blanks with victims' names and mail them the checks, which she did. She netted more than a half-million dollars, and additional fake documents were found when she was arrested. She was sentenced to 2 years in prison and 5 years probation while the scammers who hired her are still on the loose.

Calling All Units

The long and growing list of online scams leads to one question: Who is policing the internet? Well, no one. And how do interstate and international laws apply to an electronic world that has no borders? That one isn't easy to answer.

Jurisdiction and sovereignty are complicated issues in the online world. What laws, for example, apply to a person living in New York City who wants to buy a product from a European merchant whose servers are located in India?

While laws in all three locations might apply, there is an inherent conflict as to which laws take precedence, especially if the content of a website is legal in one country but not in the others. There is no current international law covering online jurisdiction.

Someone who sent money in response to a Nigerian Letter might not have broken any U.S. laws, but the person might have committed financial fraud according to Nigerian law. This type of situation actually creates a conflict of laws. The U.S. does not allow Nigerian police to enter this country and arrest someone caught in the scam, and it is difficult for U.S. law enforcement officials to prosecute scammers overseas in countries where there is lax enforcement. Overseas criminals take advantage of the naiveté of online users, many of whom don't know that the rules and laws of the country where one is online might differ from those of the U.S.

When it comes to fraud, the internet is regulated much the same as offline commerce. Someone committing online wire or credit card fraud, for example, would face the same penalties as if offline. While it gets more confusing once the fraud involves crossing states or borders, the perpetrator is at the very least liable under any local laws.

According to the IC3's 2010 Internet Crime Report, the highest number of complaints received pertaining to online fraud came from California, though only 39.1 percent of perpetrators actually lived in the state.[18]

How to Vet an Ecommerce Website

With our hectic lives, we are often multitasking online, busily checking our email while reviewing our bank account and searching Google for an affordable restaurant. While the overwhelming majority of the sites we visit are legitimate, there are always some waiting to trick us into surrendering our personal information.

These masqueraders may come in the form of an email link to a site claiming to be part of your bank, demanding your information or your account could be shut down. With others, you might stumble upon them while you're surfing the web, thinking you are going to a favorite website only to land on an authentic-looking fake created by scammers.

Ask the following questions when evaluating a commercial website:

What's your initial reaction to the site? Does it have a professional design and functionality? Does it link to real sites that in turn link back to it? Does it seem to work similarly to other sites you use to buy merchandise online? Of course, these are not foolproof signs; many scammers can afford to pump money into design—but inversely, most legitimate sites don't look amateurish.

Does the site have proper contact information? Every website should have contact information; if it doesn't, rethink doing business with the company. Check the phone number to see if it connects to the business the site purports to be. Does a receptionist answer with the name of the company and then direct you to someone? Or is it a person who sounds as if he or she just woke up from a nap? Be even more wary if there is only an automated system, and you cannot get through to a human. Is there a physical address instead of a P.O. Box? Many scammers will also use a toll-free number to try to hide their location. Do they have an email address that uses the name of the company (e.g., joe@company'sname.com as opposed to joe@yahoo.com)?

Who owns the site? Domain registration is public information. By doing a quick online search, you should uncover who registered the site and then cross-reference the information they provided (name, company address, and so on) with the information listed on the website. You can use free resources such as Whois.Net to see who registered the site. By simply typing the web address into the search engine, you should get the name, address, and contact information for the person or company that registered the website. Commercial sites aren't typically registered under the names of individuals.

What country is the website registered in? Remember, because of the difficulty in prosecuting scammers internationally, many fake sites are set up overseas. Be particularly skeptical if the site was registered in a country from which you wouldn't expect it to be operating. For instance, it would be very strange for a site claiming to be the popular H&M clothing chain to be headquartered in Sierra Leone.

What kind of payment system does the site use? Any large company will have a merchant system for processing credit cards. Check to see if there is an icon at the bottom right-hand corner of the site showing a secure and authenticated system. Most commonly, you will see the image of a padlock, which should bring up a window with the company's information and a VeriSign Trust Seal SSL certificate when clicked. Also, make sure the web address starts with "https," meaning the information is being sent over a secured server, instead of just "http," which is much easier to hack into. While many smaller merchants use sites such as PayPal to process credit cards, you should still be cautious when using this type of service. It is easy for a scammer to set up a PayPal account, and though the site provides certain minimal protection, it does not protect against the purchase of "nontangible" items such as music files or ebooks.[19]

What shows up when you do a quick web search? If you do a quick Google search for an ecommerce website, what shows up? Do you get several pages of results, including published articles about the website and other trustworthy sites linking to it? Or do you get only one or two results simply linking back to the homepage? Any business site worth its salt should have a strong Google presence, especially if the proprietors are conducting business online. Also, search for the address and phone numbers listed on the site. Do they bring up relevant search results? Does typing in the address bring up the name and Google map of the company?

Top Ten Scams

Each year the IC3 releases an Internet Crime Report.[20] The report includes the 10 most common types of online fraud. The list is meant to warn you about the most popular scams and what new trends are developing for stealing your money and/or identity. Without further ado:

1. *Non-delivery of merchandise (non-auction).* This form of fraud is fairly straightforward. It occurs when someone buys a product or service online that is never delivered. This can happen, for example, through a fraudulent craigslist post. It is very hard to know the identity of someone you are doing business with on craigslist, and if the victim pays for an item using a wire transfer there is little recourse.

Once your money is gone, it's gone, so try to purchase through sites where sellers are rated and where there is some level of protection (e.g., by using PayPal rather than sending a check or money order directly to a merchant).

2. *FBI scams.* The IC3 reported that scams using the FBI's name accounted for 13.2 percent of all crime complaints in 2010. Both the IC3 and the FBI[21] tracked several email scams in 2009 claiming to contain classified reports or documents from the agency.

One popular scam includes an email claiming to contain an FBI "Intelligence Bulletin No. 267." People who open the email are asked to download a file called "bulletin.exe," which likely contains files harmful to personal computers.

Here's a sample email posted on the FBI's website:

Intelligence Bulletin No. 267
Title: New Patterns in Al-Qaeda Financing
Date: August 15, 2009
Threat Level: Yellow (Elevated)

The Intelligence Bulletin provides law enforcement and other public safety officials with situational awareness concerning international and domestic terrorist groups and tactics.

Another fraudulent email claims to be from the FBI Counterterrorism Division and Department of Homeland Security. The email claims to contain information about a new Osama Bin Laden communication and an attached audio file of the speech, which is obviously fake, given his death in May 2011.

The audio file is usually titled something like "audio.exe." It contains software intended to steal the victim's personal information.

The FBI assures the public that it never sends unsolicited emails or reports. Internet users should never respond to, click on a link in, or open an attachment within an email claiming to be from the agency.

3. *Identity theft.* This type of fraud encompasses scams in which someone tries to steal another person's identity in order to obtain personal information, use or open a credit card in the victim's name, or access other resources in the victim's name. ID theft represented 9.8 percent of IC3's total registered complaints in 2010. For a more detailed discussion, read Chapter 2, "They Know Where You Live: Guarding Your Privacy and Identity."

One of the most popular forms of identity theft works by stealing someone's personal information online. Some techniques were described earlier in the chapter, including emails claiming to be from your bank or credit card company asking for your personal information to keep your account open, fake websites that ask for your personal information, and viruses that infect your computer via email attachments.

4. *Computer crimes.* The IC3 uses this category for scams targeting your computer. This might include spyware, viruses that wipe your memory, or someone hacking into your account.

The best way to defend against this type of fraud is to be careful what attachments you open and what links you click. If it's from a person or company you don't know, be wary. Also, try not to use networks that are not password protected. We all like to bring our laptops to the nearby café, but just be aware that if they have an open network it is possible for someone to hack into your computer.

5. *Miscellaneous fraud.* The IC3 defines this as a variety of fraud including work-at-home scams in which a company may offer you the promise of big money working from home in the hopes of selling you expensive training materials and access to referrals. The IC3 lists other popular scams that include fake sweepstakes and contests.

6. *Advance fee fraud.* This type of fraud involves messages that claim people need to pay money up front to receive some type of reward or prize. One wire fraud case in 2010 involved more than 1,000 complaints, costing victims almost $3 million, according to the IC3.

The Nigerian Letter falls into this category of scam because the victim is asked to front a small percentage of money to receive a much larger reward in return.

Again, red flags include the use of wire transfers or requesting personal banking information. As always, if the deal seems too good to be true, it probably is.

7. *Spam.* Anyone who has used email more than a couple of times is familiar with all that unwanted, unsolicited email we receive on a

daily basis. It is often imploring us to buy products from companies we've never heard of.

It is best never to respond to spam, and certainly never to give your personal information to a company or person you've never heard of. If you get an unsolicited advertisement for a product you're interested in, try to locate it through a company or online auction you are familiar with.

8. *Auction fraud.* If you are going to use an online auction site like eBay, make sure you research the company from which you are buying something. If it is from a person, check on the seller's rating within the site. By clicking on the username, you will be able to see average user ratings of the seller and how long he or she has been a member of eBay. There is also feedback from users discussing how efficiently their payment went through and how quickly they received their purchase. Avoid paying for goods through a wire transfer or personal check. A third-party site like PayPal is preferable, though even PayPal cannot always provide you full protection.

9. *Credit card fraud.* If you think someone is making unauthorized charges to your account, immediately contact your bank; a 24-hour 1-800 telephone number should appear on the back of the card.

Your liability is limited to $50 per card. If you report the card stolen before it is used, the issuer cannot hold you responsible for charges, according to the Federal Trade Commission.[22]

The same holds true for debit or ATM cards. However, unlike credit cards, the longer you wait to report the card stolen, the more money you are liable for. If you report the theft within the first 2 days, you are responsible for only $50. After 2 days, though, you can be held responsible for up to $500, and if you wait more than 60 days you risk losing the full amount of what's been charged.

Be careful where you use your cards online, and make sure to report any suspicious credit activity as soon as possible.

10. *Overpayment fraud.* This type of fraud includes the popular craigslist scams. Imagine you are trying to sell your bike on the classifieds website. You list a price of $200. A couple of days go by and you finally receive an email from an interested party. The buyer

agrees on the price and arranges to pay you via check. What arrives in the mail, though, is not a personal check but rather a cashier's check for $400. The buyer tells you they already had the check made out for something else and you can just deposit the full amount and then reimburse them.

The check appears to clear at first, but after about 3 days your bank will inform you that it's fraudulent—at which point the scammer has made off with your bike (and possibly your $200 if you've already reimbursed him).

Again, it is best to use a third party like PayPal. Be wary of checks, especially ones for an amount larger than what you're selling your item for, as this is a common means of gaining your trust.

There are more internet scams than ever, but with a little vigilance and common sense, you should be able to avoid them using the tips outlined in this chapter. To review, keep the following guidelines in mind:

- *Deal only with people you trust.* Think twice before buying something or giving your personal information to a person or company you've never heard of before. Is there a way you can vet the person or site? How legit is the website? Are you being asked to pay via a wire transfer? Is there a physical address where you can find the contact person or company if something goes wrong with the transaction? You can always check with your local consumer protection agency or the Better Business Bureau before doing business with someone.

- *Don't fall for easy money.* If it seems too good to be true, it probably is.

- *Stay away from spam.* Never give your personal information or open an attachment from an email address you are unsure of; no legitimate business will ever ask you for sensitive information over email.

- *Make certain the website is real.* You should always use caution if any site requests information such as your credit card or Social Security number. Who is the site registered to? Does the contact information match up when you do a quick Google search? Does it compare favorably with similar websites quality-wise?

- *Be careful how you pay.* Credit cards are preferable to wire transfers or debit cards online because you can always dispute the charges. Make sure you are using a secure server before inputting your card information. Check your charge account for the next couple days after your purchase to make sure there aren't any questionable charges to your account.

For further advice and assistance, visit the following websites:

- If you think you've been a victim of online fraud, you can submit a complaint to the Federal Trade Commission (www.ftccomplaintassistant.gov).

- The IC3 (www.ic3.gov) is a great resource for the latest information about online fraud.

- The Federal Trade Commission provides tips for avoiding identity theft (www.ftc.gov/bcp/edu/micro sites/idtheft/consumers/index.html).

- The U.S. Securities and Exchange Commission provides tips on avoiding internet investment scams (www.sec.gov/investor/pubs/cyberfraud.htm).

- The FBI has a resource for auction fraud (www.fbi. gov/page2/june09/auctionfraud_063009.html).

- Whois (www.whois.net) is a good site for checking who registered a domain name.

- The Better Business Bureau (www.bbb.org/us) is a great resource for vetting a company or website.

Endnotes

1. Erik Larkin, "Massive Theft of Credit Card Numbers Reported," *PC World,* January 20, 2009, accessed May 24, 2011, www.pcworld.com/article/158003/ massive_theft_of_credit_card_numbers_reported.html.

2. Brian Krebs, "Payment Processor Breach May Be Largest Ever," Washington Post.com, January 20, 2009, accessed May 24, 2011, voices.washingtonpost. com/securityfix/2009/01/payment_processor_breach_may_b.html?hpid=top news.

3. Aite Group, *Card Fraud in the United States: The Case for Encryption*, 2010, accessed May 24, 2011, www.aitegroup.com/Reports/ReportDetail.aspx? recordItemID=625.

4. Royal Canadian Mounted Police, "Credit Card Fraud Statistics and Facts," Spam Laws, accessed May 24, 2011, www.spamlaws.com/credit-fraud-stats. html.

5. U.S. Federal Trade Commission, "Resolving Specific Identity Theft Problems: Credit Cards," accessed May 24, 2011, www.ftc.gov/bcp/edu/microsites/idtheft/ consumers/resolving-specific-id-theft-problems.html#CreditCards.

6. "The 10 Minute Mind Quiz," Facebook, accessed May 24, 2011, www.face book.com/apps/application.php?id=106543466052050#!/apps/application.php? id=106543466052050&v=app_4949752878.

7. "Craigslist.org," Alexa, accessed May 24, 2011, www.alexa.com/siteinfo/craigs list.org.

8. Sydney Jones, "Online Classifieds," Pew Internet & American Life Project, May 22, 2009, accessed May 24, 2011, www.pewinternet.org/Reports/2009/7-- Online-Classifieds.aspx. Also see www.craiglist.org/about/factsheet for statistical information.

9. *United States of America v. Svechinskaya et al.* Case 1:10-mj-02137-UA-1filed in United States District Court, Southern District of New York in Manhattan on September 28, 2010.

10. Tim Hanrahan, "Scotland Yard Shuts Down Scam Sites," *Wall Street Journal,* December 3, 2009, accessed July 19, 2011, online.wsj.com/article/SB10001424 052748704007804574573943476575018.html.

11. "Trend Data," Pew Internet & American Life Project, May 2011, accessed June 2, 2011, www.pewinternet.org/Trend-Data/Online-Activites-Total.aspx.

12. "2010 Annual Report on Internet Crime," Internet Crime Complaint Center, February 24, 2011, accessed June 2, 2011, www.ic3.gov/media/2011/110224. aspx.

13. "2010 Internet Crime Report," Internet Crime Complaint Center, accessed June 2, 2011, www.ic3.gov/media/annualreport/2010_IC3Report.pdf.

14. "Internet Crime Schemes," Internet Crime Complaint Center, accessed May 24, 2011, www.ic3.gov/crimeschemes.aspx.

15. "Common Fraud Schemes," FBI, accessed May 24, 2011, www.fbi.gov/maj cases/fraud/fraudschemes.htm.

16. "Nigerian 419 Email Scam," Fight Identity Theft, accessed May 24, 2011, www.fightidentitytheft.com/internet_scam_nigerian.html.

17. *United States of America v. Edna Fiedler*, Case 3:08-cr-05032-BHS-001 filed in United States District Court, Western District of Washington in Tacoma on January 16, 2008.

18. "2010 Internet Crime Report."

19. "PayPal User Agreement," PayPal, last updated November 1, 2010, accessed May 24, 2011, cms.paypal.com/us/cgi-bin/?&cmd=_render-content&content_ID=ua/UserAgreement_full&locale.x=en_US.

20. "2010 Annual Report on Internet Crime."

21. "New E-Scams & Warnings," FBI, accessed May 24, 2011, www.fbi.gov/cyber invest/escams.htm.

22. "Facts for Consumers," U.S. Federal Trade Commission, June 2002, accessed May 24, 2011, www.ftc.gov/bcp/edu/pubs/consumer/credit/cre04.shtm.

CHAPTER 5

Information Warfare and Cybersecurity

Deborah A. Liptak

Tokyo Rose
Date: August 14, 1944, 8:30 PM
Location: South Pacific
Event: The "Zero Hour," an English-language Japanese broadcast of war news, popular American music, and Japanese propaganda, is broadcast to the Allied Forces. The familiar voice of Tokyo Rose is heard over the radio waves:

> Hello you fighting orphans in the Pacific. How's tricks? This is "After her weekend, and oooh, back on the air, strictly under union hours." Reception okay? Why, it better be, because this is All-Requests night. And I've got a pretty nice program for my favorite little family, the wandering bone-heads of the Pacific Islands. The first request is made by none other than the boss. And guess what? He wants Bonnie Baker in "My Resistance is Low." My, what taste you have, sir, she says.[1]

The persona of Tokyo Rose is a well-known example of information warfare (IW) from World War II. This propaganda scheme by the Japanese government was not very effective at dissuading the American troops who looked forward to the nightly broadcasts in hopes of hearing their favorite American music, and it definitely wasn't taken lightly. Iva Toguri D'Aquino was one of the many voices broadcast to the Allied Troops during World War II, voices that were collectively known as Tokyo Rose. A Japanese-American woman, D'Aquino was tried and convicted of treason in 1949 and served 6 years in prison.

Warfare in the Age of Information

From the ringing alarm clock at the beginning of our day to late-night news and entertainment, information about our world bombards us in a variety of formats. We read books, newspapers, and magazines. We watch television, movies, plays, and other forms of entertainment. We listen to cell phones, music, and radio. We surf the internet through a multitude of connected devices for a variety of reasons, such as online banking, investing, and engaging in commerce.

As citizens of the 21st century, we swim in information, we are overloaded by it, our lives revolve around it, and our livelihoods depend on it. Following World War II, our information sources and communications systems became increasingly linked to computers and invisible electronic transmissions that move in waves through cyberspace much the same as the "ether" that long-ago philosophers thought filled the vacuum of space.

War has been around as long as humankind; there are more than 1,000 wars on record. Communication in warfare has always been vital to military operations, and information—or lack of information—has historically often meant the difference between victory and defeat in battles and in wars. We once fought only on the land, sea, and air, but technology has expanded the battlefield to include space and information zones. Increasingly sophisticated weapon systems depend upon information, and specifically on electronic information. Information has many functions beyond gaining knowledge about the enemy. In this capacity, new technologies make hunting and gathering more possible and more necessary.

The U.S. military created the internet in the 1960s using leased commercial communications lines and equipment—the same systems used by the private sector for communications. Because of these shared communications links between private sectors and government organizations, the "communications zone," traditionally maintained in the rear part of a theater of war, is no longer a fixed, centralized place. The communications zone has blurred with the shared use of information infrastructures by the military and civilians.

Government and private-sector targets are often the same. Search the news database of your choice, and you will find countless reports and examples of IW, from cell phone jamming to denial of service (DoS), spam attacks, and phishing schemes. It may seem far removed from our individual lives, but it affects us all at a national level.

Defining IW

IW has been around since the first war, in the forms of intelligence, public opinion, propaganda, rumors, innuendo, misinformation, and deception, to name a few. When the U.S. emerged from the Cold War in 1991 as the dominant world power, the term *information warfare* also emerged in the literature, perhaps due to the increasing interdependency of communications systems with other infrastructures. Information superiority, or dominance, became the ultimate goal of IW. Because IW is still an emerging concept, experts disagree on its exact definition as well as the parts or components involved. The term came along with dozens of other colorful names describing post-Cold War hostile activities. Asymmetrical warfare, electronic warfare, netwar or netcentric warfare, cyberwar, cyberterrorism, and cyberattack are among the terms frequently encountered when studying IW:

> In the end, it hardly matters which "cyber" label we use— cyberterrorism, cyberwarfare, cybercrime or cyberattacks— as long as we pay attention to these early warning signs. We know terrorist groups are focused on building IT skills and investing in computer science education for their followers. We hope they'll never launch a successful cyberattack, but they'll certainly try.[2]

IW can be described as both offensive and defensive operations, similar to the way a football game is played. Information can be both a weapon and a target, used to attack an enemy and/or to defend oneself. Offensive operations are designed to disrupt the enemy's information systems, while defensive operations are designed to protect friendly information systems.

Leigh Armistead's *Information Operations: The Hard Reality of Soft Power*, a textbook used by the Joint Forces Staff College and the National Security Agency, lists six elements of IW: computer network attack, deception, destruction, electronic warfare, operations security, and psychological operations.[3]

Military Information Operations

Government computers are hacked on a daily basis. Information security—protecting information and information systems against unauthorized access, modification, or DoS—is an essential component of information operations (IO).

George A. Crawford, lieutenant colonel (retired) of the U.S. Air Force, gave an account in the fall 1995 issue of *Air & Space Power Chronicles* of a successful IO campaign from Operation Desert Storm, the 1991 U.S. invasion of Kuwait to liberate it from Iraq:

> In order to gain air supremacy, a joint special operations aviation force opened a breach in radar coverage surrounding Iraq. The Iraqi command was unaware the breach existed until a blow had been struck from which Iraq would never recover. Simultaneously, a coordinated attack by stealth aircraft against Iraq's air defense headquarters bunker and three regional air defense centers effectively turned Iraq's integrated air defense network into a hodgepodge of uncoordinated air defense fiefdoms, each of which could be neutralized independently at the coalition forces' leisure. No longer did a surface-to-air missile site have a regional C2 system to prioritize and provide early warning of approaching targets. Later in the campaign, a baited hook was thrown to news agencies when reporters—desperate for a story—were allowed to cover exercises in preparation for an amphibious assault into Kuwait. This successful psychological operation by a Marine Amphibious Brigade and Navy special forces held five Iraqi divisions in place on the east coast while two corps of coalition forces shifted to the western flank for the final assault.[4]

Armistead explained that the six elements of IW are also IO capabilities that take place during peacetime.[5] IO also involves the two related activities of public affairs and civil affairs:

Many military theorists contend that IW is what you do when IO fails. That is one difference but there are also subtleties between these two warfare areas as well. The difference between these two terms is that IW contains six elements and is mostly involved with the conduct of operations during actual combat, while IO on the other hand, includes these six capabilities and two sometimes integrated or related activities. IO is broader than IW and is intended to be conducted as a strategic campaign throughout the full spectrum of conflict from peace to war and back to peace. Therefore IO is much more comprehensive than IW and it is in IO that the full integration across government agencies and with private industry must occur.[6]

The military is the premier authority for IO when it comes to the objective of disrupting enemy IO while defending and protecting friendly IO. While the military is the professional in handling "real" IO and warfare, there are lessons to be learned by anyone with enemies, whether competitors or disgruntled former or current employees. The Cyberspace and Information Operations Study Center experts at the U.S. Air Force's Air University, Air War College, have compiled more than 200 online pages of information and active links called "Information Operations, Warfare, Info Ops, Infowar, Cyberwar" (www.au.af.mil/info-ops) that explains the intimate, unclassified details of IO.[7]

IW Attacks: Who and Why

A variety of individuals and groups are involved in IW attacks. Hackers, usually working alone, and "hacktivists," working either alone or in a group to promote a cause, are probably the best-known wagers of everyday IW. These intruders enter computer systems to prove they can enter undetected, steal passwords and information, corrupt data, or even destroy systems. During the Bosnian conflict in the late 1990s, IW was waged against North Atlantic Treaty Organization (NATO) nations by hackers. Author Kevin Maney believes these hackers were amateurs who caused minimal damage. "After NATO began bombing Serbia in 1999, Serbian-sympathizing hackers from all over the world attacked more than 100 businesses in

NATO nations. It had less impact on daily life than a broken traffic light."[8]

A rather ominous report documents a trend that bears watching. Sociologists Diego Gambetta and Steffen Hertog surveyed more than 400 terrorists. They discovered that 44 percent were engineers—so-called unemployed techies—who were recruited for terror operations.[9]

News agencies reported cyberattacks in 2009 and 2010 in Estonia and Georgia. The finger of responsibility for these disruptive acts has pointed to Russia.

In addition to these cyberattacks, other nations have been accused of IW:

- A hacker believed to reside in China infiltrated Pentagon computers and government computers in Britain, Germany, India, and Australia.

- Sophisticated attacks involved hackers in Israel and Palestine, India and Pakistan, the U.S. and China, and Pakistan and Afghanistan.[10] National governments and their foreign intelligence services, both friendly and hostile, gather intelligence information daily. Many foreign nations have IW capabilities. China and Russia have been in the news in recent years for developing IW techniques.

A 2008 Incident

According to Aaron Mannes and James Hendler of the U.K.'s *Guardian*, "The Russian–Georgian conflict is being described as the first time cyberattacks have accompanied an actual war."[11]

The 2008 South Ossetia war, also known as the Russia–Georgia War, included hacking of local servers and distributed denial of service (DDoS). In August 2008, while much of the world focused its attention on the XXIX Summer Olympics in Beijing, Russian troops concerned about political turmoil in South Ossetia, Georgia, invaded Tskhinvali and Abkhazia. By August 8, most Georgian media and government websites were shut down by DDoS attacks. "It was the internet version of the blitzkrieg, and a blow to military and civilian morale in Georgia."[12] Richard McEachin of McEachin & Associates Ltd. reported: "Civil.ge, the Georgian news site, is under cyberattack by the Russians."[13] Their content "was moved to Google's Blogspot to keep the information flowing about what's going on in Georgia. Google has the infrastructure and resources to defend against these attacks."[14]

According to *The Register*, "Security researchers from Grey-logic published a report on Friday (March 20, 2009) which concluded Russia's Foreign Military Intelligence agency (the GRU) and Federal Security Service (the FSB), rather than patriotic hackers, were likely to have played a key role in co-ordinating and organising the attacks."[15]

A *Los Angeles Times* editorial on August 17, 2008, summarized the current vulnerabilities of the internet infrastructure:

> The internet was not designed to be secure. Its architecture was developed by a relatively small group of researchers who knew and trusted one another. They didn't envision the Net becoming intertwined with commerce, manufacturing and the power grid, all of which are now to some degree vulnerable to cyber warriors ... Georgia's experience serves as a warning to internet users that war has been redefined to the detriment of civilians everywhere.[16]

2009 Incidents

According to various newspaper articles, including some in the *Wall Street Journal,* Kyrgyzstan experienced DoS attacks on January 18, 2009, that were believed to originate with a Russian "cybermilitary" organization.[17] Two main internet service providers were targeted, an attack that used 80 percent of Kyrgyzstan's bandwidth.

On May 1, 2009, the Liberation Tigers of Tamil Eelam hacked into the Sri Lankan army's and Sri Lanka government's websites. Hackers inserted gruesome pictures. The websites were quickly restored.

The Iranian government uses software to filter and censor what its citizens read online. On June 16, 2009, during Iranian election protests, the Iranian government discovered its citizens were coordinating protests using social media technology such as Twitter and imposed its own DoS.[18]

According to the *Wall Street Journal,* from July 4 to 9, 2009, DDoS and botnet (commonly malicious software robots that run autonomously and automatically) cyberattacks occurred against South Korean and U.S. websites. The attacks included the U.S. White House, Department of Homeland Security, and State Department, as well as the New York Stock Exchange, U.S. Bankcorp, and the *Washington Post.* Similar sites were affected in South Korea. The government of North Korea is the prime suspect.[19]

On July 10, 2009, Israel National News reported that Israel Defense Forces and Iran were already engaged in cyberwar.[20]

2010 Incidents

The Stuxnet computer worm, the first known self-replicating worm designed to take over industrial supervisory control and data acquisition software, was detected in June 2010. Since its discovery, Stuxnet has spread worldwide to factories, electric power plants, and transmission systems, with Iran sustaining an estimated 60 percent of the attacks, including software at the Bushehr nuclear power plant. Due to the level of sophistication of the Stuxnet worm, cyberexperts argue it might be the work of a state. In response to the worm, an Iranian spokesperson claimed, "An electronic war has been launched against Iran."[21] See the Introduction for more information on Stuxnet.

Ireland's Central Applications Office (CAO; www.cao.ie) is the organization responsible for overseeing most undergraduate college applications in the Republic of Ireland. CAO was the victim of a DoS attack on August 23, 2010, 10 minutes after offers were placed online, leaving about 23,000 applicants distraught and distressed for more than 7 hours. The source of the malicious attack was unknown, and the CAO website had been previously targeted on July 1, 2010, the deadline for change-of-mind applications.[22]

According to Symantec MessageLabs Intelligence analysis for August 2010, the proportion of spam sent from botnets increased to about 95 percent by the end of July 2010. The Grum botnet, the dominant spambot in 2009, significantly decreased. Analysis of the spike in spam being sent from other sources suggests that it was actually being sent from an unclassified variant of the Rustock botnet. Rustock remained the most dominant spam-sending botnet in August 2010, responsible for more than 41 percent of all spam. Yet Rustock actually shrank from about 2.5 million bots under its control in April 2010 to about 1.3 million in August 2010.[23]

When 40 Pakistani websites came under cyberattack by the Indian Cyber Army, Pakistani "Predators PK" retaliated against India's Central Bureau of Investigation. The cyberwar started in 1998 and has intensified.[24]

WikiLeaks is a nonprofit organization that publishes untraceable mass documents for the purpose of whistleblowing and leaking.[25] In 2010, WikiLeaks released an estimated half-million classified documents concerning the wars in Iraq and Afghanistan. Many critics, including the U.S. State Department, considered these actions to be acts of cyberwar. Our definition of cyberwar differs from the point of view of these critics. However, a hacktivist group known as "Anonymous" did launch a DDoS attack called "Operation: Payback" against several companies who withdrew support for WikiLeaks. These companies included major financial institutions, online stores, and social media websites.[26]

2011 Incidents

Educated and technically skilled Egyptian activists protested the regime of President Hosni Mubarak on the cyberspace pages of Facebook and Twitter. Mubarak's loyal supporters retaliated; in addition to bloody clashes on the streets of Cairo, a shouting match in cyberspace ensued. "On January 28, Egypt's four main internet service providers cut off access to their customers in a bid to break the momentum of the demonstrations. It was restored five days later after the ban attracted global condemnation."[27] More than a quarter of the Egyptian population (23 million people) were affected by this internet blackout, costing Egypt an estimated $18 million per day. Facebook expressed concern; Google and Twitter created a tool allowing Egyptians to bypass the internet and post messages to Twitter by phone.

During a keynote address, Sri Lanka's army commander said that the 30-year physical civil war has ended, but cyberwar is still being waged by terrorists, including a web defacement attack. The commander pointed out that countering the cyberwar is the responsibility of every sector. "In combating this, all of us, service providers, banking sector, manufacturing sector, government sector together with armed forces must become soldiers and warriors before [we have] been victims of it," the army chief said.[28]

In late April 2011 the Iranian government announced the detection of a new hostile computer virus, the Stars Virus, which damages government computers by mimicking an executable file.[29]

Other Attacks

Espionage is not limited to governments. Insiders, disgruntled employees, and even trusted clients can all gather and harvest information. Terrorist groups such as Al-Qaida conduct IW. Libya was accused of cyberterrorism in 2005 when it jammed allied radio transmissions. Criminal groups who perpetrate scams or phish for money are growing by leaps and bounds. Virus writers can be included in this same group. Spam floods our email inboxes daily, causing us to spend time filtering the wheat from the chaff and watching for malicious viruses. The following are more examples of varied cyberthreats:

- Online hackers calling themselves "Anonymous" reportedly attacked the Church of Scientology's website using DDoS on January 19, 2008. The church retaliated by moving its domain to Prolexic Technologies, a company that specializes in protecting websites from DoS attacks.[30]

- Rep. Duncan Hunter's 2008 presidential campaign website, GoHunter08.com, was briefly hacked by an attacker in Turkey, "Adnali for Turkstorm.Org."[31]

- The Defense Department took as many as 1,500 Pentagon computers offline on Thursday, June 21, 2007, because of a cyberattack.[32]

- In April 2008, Radio Free Europe was knocked offline for 3 days due to a cyberattack that was a protest against planned coverage of Belarusian demonstrations on the 22nd anniversary of the Chernobyl nuclear accident. The DDoS attack involved more than 50,000 messages per second. Belarusian leader Alyaksandr Lukashenka is a suspect, but his regime has not been positively identified with the attacks.

- The website of the United Civil Front, a Russian opposition political party led by former Russian chess star Gary Kasparov, was repeatedly knocked offline by DDoS attacks for 2 weeks in December 2007.

- In April 2007, patriotic Chinese hackers retaliated against the CNN news coverage of Tibet with a DDoS. The attack failed to bring down CNN because the site's administrators were aware of the plans and were prepared for the attack.

- Since 2002, Tibetan activists have received hundreds of malicious software emails a month disguised as PowerPoint presentations or other materials. In truth, these emails are Trojan programs that spy on the user's PC and relay information back to the malware's author.

- Pentagon officials believe that Chinese cyberspies accessed their networks in September 2007 and stole an unknown number of the Department of Defense's emails. To secure the network, many Pentagon computers were shut down for more than a week. Prime military contractors were also hacked from computers based in China.

- Several days before the 2008 Pennsylvania presidential primary, the community blogs section of Barack Obama's campaign website redirected users to Hillary Clinton's site. This is called pagejacking and violates federal law.

The Targets

The internet as we know it today is only a small portion of the National Information Infrastructure (NII), which interconnects communications networks, computers, databases, and consumer electronics. This infrastructure includes a wide range of equipment in the audio and video spectrum through human/machine interface devices, both individual and networked. The people managing and operating the transmission of information are a critical component of the infrastructure. It is made up of eight automated and interlinked critical infrastructures, targeted by physical and cyberattacks:

- Electrical power systems

- Information and communications

- Gas and oil

- Banking and finance

- Transportation

- Water supply

- Government services

- Emergency services

The NII was initiated by the Clinton administration in 1995 after the destruction of Pan American Flight 103 over Lockerbie, Scotland (December 21, 1988), the World Trade Center attack (February 23, 1993), the bombing of the Murrah Federal Building in Oklahoma City (April 19, 1995), and numerous computer attacks against government and private sector business and commerce.

In addition to the NII, the Department of Defense has its own interconnected Defense Information Infrastructure called the Global Information Grid. Both the NII and the Defense Information Infrastructure interface with the Global Information Infrastructure. It is often uncertain where one ends and the other begins.

After the attacks on September 11, 2001, much was written about vulnerabilities in the U.S. communications systems. News coverage reported that radio communications used by the New York City Fire Department failed to work before, during, and after the collapse of the World Trade Center towers. It is less widely known that suburban New York, New Jersey, and Connecticut fire departments met at central locations outside New York City waiting for the call from the New York City Fire Department to proceed to the disaster area as part of a prearranged disaster preparedness plan in case of a catastrophic event within the city. The calls never came to proceed to the disaster area, delaying supplementary professional rescue help for hours.

The U.S. information infrastructure is also vulnerable to attack at the node and router levels. Attackers range from the novice to the sophisticated. Sensitive information is exposed and data corrupted, while DoS prevents legitimate users from accessing essential information. Attack detection has been thoroughly studied, but little effort has been spent designing the infrastructure architecture to effectively manage responses to attacks.[33]

Electrical Grid

Countries are also vulnerable to attacks on electrical grids. While not an example of illegal activity or an intentional cyberattack, the events of August 14, 2003, illustrate this vulnerability, as parts of the Northeast U.S. and Canada experienced a major power failure at the electrical grid level. Cell phones were disrupted (wired telephones worked, to the surprise of many people). News in nonprint formats vanished. Radio stations returned to the air by using backup power systems, but listeners had replaced transistor radios, used during blackouts of old, with CD players and newer devices. Cable television systems did not work once power was restored to homes unless power had also been restored to the cable provider. Internet users were disconnected from their news sources for the duration of the blackout, with the exception of dial-up access from laptop computers, which worked as long as the battery charges lasted. Emergency communications systems depended on volunteer amateur radio operators to relay information during the outage.[34]

In 2009, President-elect Obama asked the U.S. Congress "to build a new smart grid that will save us money, protect our power sources from blackout or attack, and deliver clean, alternative forms of energy to every corner of our nation."[35] Although the U.S. has one of the most reliable electric grids in the world, the U.S. Energy Department was quick to point out that a rare "high-impact, low-frequency event," including a coordinated cyberattack on the system, could cause long-term, catastrophic damage to our electrical infrastructure.[36]

Emergency Communications Systems

Another event that triggered national response and fury concerned the lack of communications before, during, and after Hurricane Katrina struck the coastal areas of Louisiana, Alabama, and Mississippi on August 29, 2005. Because the critical information and telecommunications system is geographically concentrated, it is particularly vulnerable to natural disasters and terrorist attacks. Hurricanes Katrina and Rita (also in 2005) disrupted the energy as well as the communications infrastructures. Hurricane Katrina will long be remembered as a time of bad information, lack of information, and information and communications systems that just didn't work. Older communications systems once again proved their worth, and alternative communications systems provided creative ways for survivors to deal with the disaster. Water and high winds damaged centralized communications systems, hindering rescue efforts.

During the "Saffron Revolution" (September 28 through October 1, 2007), Burmese anti-government protests resulted in the government of Myanmar (aka Burma) cutting internet access. Evidence of the violent crackdown on monks and other demonstrators was recorded by "netizens" using various online technologies to communicate with friends, loved ones, and the media.

The Myanmar and Iranian cyberattacks against Twitter during the 2009 election were cases of government censorship against their own citizens. Both the Burmese military junta and the Iranian government severed the internet connection throughout their countries in an attempt to suppress demonstrators and protesters communicating with the outside world.

A May 2007 attack on Estonian websites came from Russian hackers retaliating against Estonia for relocating a Russian war memorial. With Estonia's reliance on computer networks for government and business, the 3-week coordinated attack proved to be disruptive. The DoS attacks in Kyrgyzstan during January 2009 are also believed to be retaliatory because of Kyrgyzstan's agreement with the U.S. to host an airbase. Russian citizens were believed to have originated both attacks.

Georgia and Sri Lanka experienced cyberwar in conjunction with acts of physical war. The Russia–Georgia War was well-timed by the Russians to coordinate with the Olympics in August 2008, while the eyes of the world were riveted on Beijing. Similarly, the Sri Lankan cyberwar of May 2009 was carried out in conjunction with a vicious civil war.

The July 2009 cyberattacks against South Korea and the U.S. began on July 4, a long weekend in the U.S. While considered minor by most experts, these attacks had the potential to be serious. They involved government websites including the White House, the Pentagon, the State Department, and the New York Stock Exchange. Many organizations, including government agencies, have a reduced staff at night and on weekends. Theoretically, if the attack had been more severe, it might have taken longer to repair and caused more of a morale problem.

Because the internet is faceless, cyberattacks are difficult to trace, and it was nearly impossible to know whether the attacks originated from North Korea or South Korea. John Markoff of the *New York Times* reported that "the internet was effectively a 'wilderness of mirrors,' and ... attributing the source of cyberattacks and other kinds of exploitation is difficult at best and sometimes impossible."[37]

IW Attacks: When and Where

The experts don't necessarily agree on when and where future attacks of IW will take place. They also don't agree about how severe these attacks might be, either. Several years ago, information experts were comparing IW to "an electronic Pearl Harbor." Predictions circulated that an enemy state or terrorist group might launch a surprise attack in cyberspace that would incapacitate the U.S. Such predictions caused many people to become fearful. Former Central Intelligence Agency director George Tenet told a Senate hearing in 1998, "Information warfare has the potential to deal a crippling blow to our national security if we do not take strong measures to counter it."[38] Tenet's words sound strikingly similar to thoughts echoed by today's political and military leaders.

We may be attacked when we least expect it. Writer Dan Verton believes the next terrorist attack on the U.S. would be closely followed by a physical or cyberattack on electrical power systems and information and communications systems. This would hinder rescue efforts.[39]

We may be assaulted constantly. Writer John Swartz describes an attack where "hundreds of powerful computers at the Defense Department and U.S. Senate were hijacked by hackers who used them to send spam email."[40]

Kevin Maney, along with many other experts, believes that a coordinated attack by another nation is a cause for worry. "There's more chance such an attack could shut down or clog not only military computers, but financial networks and other systems that run the U.S. economy."[41]

Some experts don't think the threat is as widespread as the media may portray it, but vigilance is necessary. Computer security expert Bruce Schneier believes that most of what we think of as IW is associated with criminal activity. "Hacking has moved from a hobbyist pursuit with a goal of notoriety to a criminal pursuit with a goal of money."[42] Schneier's position on the severity of hacking and the information warfare threat is antithetical to George Crawford's 1995 assumption that, "Although information itself will not cost lives, denial or subversion of that information may lead to lives lost."[43]

IW Attacks: How

There are a wide variety of ways to attack information and other infrastructure systems (also see Appendix B):

- Abuse of privilege
- Criminal (spamming, spoofing, phishing, hacking)
- DoS, DDoS, packet sniffer, jamming
- Eavesdropping, wiretapping, keyboard acoustic emanations, tracking of mobile phones
- Electromagnetic pulse
- Espionage (corporate and domestic), spyware
- Exploit tools
- Hacking (information modification)
- Logic bombs
- Masquerade, misauthentication
- Network flooding, pinging
- System malfunction or modification
- Theft of information or service

- Viruses (Trojan horses, worms, logic bombs)

- Vishing (phishing based on Voice over Internet Protocol technology and open source call center software)

- Unauthorized access or use of resources

- War-dialing or war-driving

- Zero-day exploit

Being Proactive About IW

The 2006 AT&T Business Continuity Study found that more than 25 percent of U.S. companies were unprepared for disasters. Only 28 percent of information technology executives participating in the 2006 study consider cybersecurity to be a top concern.[44]

AT&T's 2008 Business Continuity Study shows a significant change over the 2-year period from 2006. In 2008, nearly 50 percent of all companies had implemented specific protective actions after the federal or state government issued an alert for an impending disaster. A total of 55 percent of information technology executives viewed cybersecurity as a concern, and 74 percent of executives indicated that cybersecurity was part of their company's overall business continuity plan.[45]

Sadly, the March 2006 Computer Security Report Card, prepared by the Committee on Government Reform, and based on reports required by the Federal Information Security Management Act of 2002, gave an overall government rating of D+ to government computers in 2005.

The Eighth Report Card on Computer Security, issued in May 2008, gave an overall rating of C to government computers in 2007. This report measured a small overall improvement over a 2-year period, but this was not nearly enough to keep our government computers safe.

What Not to Do: The Case of the Department of Homeland Security

A May 2004 study by the U.S. Government Accountability Office (GAO) recommends three broad actions the federal government can take to encourage the use of cybersecurity technologies: 1) help critical infrastructures determine their cybersecurity needs, 2) model behavior by protecting its own systems, and 3) undertake activities to increase the quality and availability of cybersecurity technologies in the marketplace. However, the GAO also places critical infrastructure protection responsibilities on the critical infrastructure owners. Cybersecurity is the user's responsibility.[46]

Teamwork between the government and the private sector is essential to ensure the cybersecurity of the U.S. The Department of Homeland Security (DHS) began several initiatives to coordinate a public/private plan for internet recovery but made limited progress. In June 2006, the GAO published the report "DHS Faces Challenges in Developing a Joint Public/Private Recovery Plan." The GAO outlined five key challenges that the DHS must overcome to achieve results in implementing an internet disaster recovery plan. Several of these challenges sound similar to the problems DHS encountered during the Hurricane Katrina crisis:

- Innate characteristics of the internet that make planning for and responding to disruptions difficult

- Lack of consensus on DHS's role and when the department should get involved in responding to a disruption

- Legal issues affecting DHS's ability to provide assistance to restore internet service

- Reluctance of many private sector organizations to share information on internet disruptions with DHS

- Leadership and organizational uncertainties within DHS[47]

On September 10, 2007, the GAO made further recommendations to the DHS "to develop a strategy for coordinating control systems security efforts and to enhance information sharing with relevant stakeholders. DHS officials did not agree or disagree with GAO's recommendations, but stated that they would take them under advisement." To the casual observer, it didn't appear that much had been resolved in three years.[48]

A year later, on September 16, 2008, the GAO clearly indicated that since 2005, "GAO has previously made about 30 recommendations to help DHS fulfill its cybersecurity responsibilities and resolve underlying challenges. DHS in large part concurred with GAO's recommendations and in many cases has actions planned and underway to implement them." However, the report title says it all: "DHS Needs to Better Address Its Cybersecurity Responsibilities."[49]

While we wait for the DHS to decide how and when to act on the advice of the GAO, it is important that your own organization remain proactive: Fight IW. Mark Loos of the SANS Institute for computer security training provided four basic steps in a detailed checklist format for implementing a local computer security program that is still useful today.[50] A very detailed checklist can be found at www.sans.org/reading_room/whitepapers/warfare/ under "Implementing a Local Security Program to Protect National Infrastructure System Companies and Facili."

Defensive Fighting, Offensive Reacting

Information security is the protection of information and information systems against attacks and the means necessary to detect, document, and counter such attacks. It is composed of computer security and communications security. Communications security denies access to unauthorized people, ensures the authenticity of telecommunications, and includes cryptosecurity, transmission security, emission security, traffic-flow security, and physical security. As a potential target for attack, try to cover all possible vulnerabilities for your organization and be constantly on alert to danger, damage, or theft. "Defensive information warfare is a tough job."[51]

The Vulnerability Assessment and Mitigation Methodology developed by the RAND Corporation (www.rand.org/pubs/monograph_reports/2005/MR1601.pdf) provides a comprehensive review of vulnerabilities and maps the vulnerabilities to specific security techniques to correct them.[52]

Julie Huff, a systems architect at PRC, a division of Northrup Grumman, believes in offensive measures against computer attacks. "What we wanted to offer was not another form of intrusion detection, but a way to respond."[53] Writer Deborah Radcliff covered challenges involved in counterattacks in a 2000 *Computerworld* article.

While the technology products mentioned are dated, the article contains valid points to consider before striking out as an information warrior. Liability and legal issues, national and international law, and possible civil and criminal charges all must be considered. Traces must occur during a live connection. Tracing the attack route may constitute trespassing and could actually violate the attacker's privacy. In the private sector, there are restrictions on this sort of activity. Criminal suits are difficult to prosecute, and security expert Ira Winkler provides pointers for gathering your own evidence, such as tracking an attack to the IP address, using caution to not alter the data. Richard Power, an editor at the Computer Security Institute, suggests that if a crime is reported to law enforcement authorities, be prepared with an estimated monetary cost of the crime, which may vary by jurisdiction.[54]

Redundancy, Backups, and Alternative Methods of Communications

Natural disasters can teach us lessons about survivable communications and information systems. Unfortunately, they occur on a regular basis. Domestic terrorist attacks, fortunately, are still fairly rare. Traditional telephone and transistor radios worked effectively after many disasters. In September 1979, Hurricane Fred knocked out modern communications systems on the Mississippi Gulf Coast. Alternative forms of communications were used for several hours, primarily short-wave radio transmissions from amateur ham radio operators.

During the National Conference on Emergency Communications at George Washington University in December 2005, Dennis Wingo, the president of Assured Power and Communications, stated, "It all goes back to making do with what you have."[55]

Alternative modes of communications, especially blogs, wikis, and other digital resources, are evolving and responding as optional methods of communications during emergencies. Considering how fragile communications systems are and the negative impact on morale and life that miscommunications and the loss of communications can have, it is advisable to examine alternative methods to communicate.[56]

Redundancy in telecommunications and information systems and backup power sources are critical. Because the communications and information infrastructure are so dependent on electricity, the energy infrastructure becomes essential for telecommunications and information systems. These three systems may be the most critical to keep running before, during, and after a cyberattack. "When backups for damaged components are not readily available (e.g., extra high voltage transformers for the electric power grid), such damage could have a long-lasting effect."[57]

Centralized telephone system switches can comfortably accommodate about 10 percent of their customers at any time. Outages can occur if the system is overloaded, as happens during a crisis. Cell phone circuits failed during the New York City blackout of 2003. Flooding during and after Hurricane Katrina destroyed underground phone lines, and high winds tore down cell phone towers. The power grid for large areas of the Gulf Coast was also affected, denying electricity to phone systems.

On the other hand, Wi-Fi networks are decentralized, inexpensive, and use low power. They can provide alternative communications and even provide backup for a phone system during a disaster. Wi-Fi nodes built onto houses or buildings could share internet connections and handle Voice over Internet Protocol phone calls. Their decentralized construction allows a single node to collapse without destroying the network.

High-density areas such as cities should have a backup communications system. Nodes are less likely than cell phone towers to be affected by high winds. They are vulnerable to power loss, but a backup battery could keep each node running (a standard 400-amp deep-discharge battery can supply a DSL modem/wireless router for about 20 days). Wi-Fi networks are a realistic way to maintain communications, especially with rescue services and the outside world.[58]

Since Hurricane Katrina, municipalities may be financially justified in investing in neighborhood backup systems for power and/or duplicate communication. Self-sufficient neighborhoods with "local power generation and redundant networks and services, could be achieved with technology changes that are on the horizon." However, defining the boundaries of a neighborhood is one of the challenges associated with this concept.[59]

The Chicago-based Center for Neighborhood Technology (wcn. cnt.org/about) is assisting households with Wi-Fi mesh installations, including a node in Rayville, Louisiana. New Orleans has already begun to take steps toward installing and running a free municipal internet system based on Wi-Fi technology. Included in that citywide network are secure communications for police and fire departments.[60]

Into the Future

The threat of IW increased with the events of September 11, 2001, and the subsequent war against terrorism on the Afghan, Iraqi, and U.S. homefronts. Indeed, the fronts themselves are shifting, as IW is not confined to a geographical location but waged in the invisible spectrum of cyberspace. The media, in its endeavor to sell the news, has most likely exploited IW, sensationalizing it to the point where it is hard to discern the truth.

How has IW changed in the decades since Tokyo Rose? While propaganda campaigns continue via the internet as well as radio, television, and print media, we find that intentional attacks on networks, computers, and their increasing interaction within various infrastructures occur much more frequently. Here's how it might look today:

Date: December 7, 2011, 10:00 AM, the 70th Anniversary of Pearl Harbor
Location: A Downtown Cybercafé
Event: The "Coffee Break," during which video, social media, news podcasts, MP3 music, and pop-up spam are transmitted through the local Wi-Fi node. Real information seems to be crawling like a snail through cold molasses. These familiar offers are seen on notebook screens and handheld devices:

> Hello Dear, Get your meds online
> Live Video Cam Chat!
> Would you like an extra $5,000 a month in income?
> We can refinance your house at a lower rate
> Be great in bed—Vi*gr* Cheap
> Wall Street Alert! This stock is about to Zoom
> Notice - PayPal Account Limited
> Rolex, Lous Vuitton replica
> Adobe software …

Endnotes

1. "'Hello, You Fighting Orphans': 'Tokyo Rose' Woos U.S. Sailors and Marines," History Matters, accessed June 3, 2011, historymatters.gmu.edu/d/5140.

2. Maryfran Johnson, "CyberWhoCares IT Should!," *Computerworld,* December 2, 2002, 24.

3. Joint Command, Control & Information Operations School, *Information Operations: The Hard Reality of Soft Power*, Joint Forces Staff College, accessed June 3, 2011, www.jfsc.ndu.edu/schools_programs/jc2ios/io/io_text book.pdf.

4. George A. Crawford, "Information Warfare: New Roles for Information Systems in Military Operations," Maxwell AFB Alabama, Air University, *Air & Space Power Chronicles*, Fall 1995, accessed June 3, 2011, www.iwar.org.uk/iwar/resources/airchronicles/crawford.htm.

5. Joint Command, Control & Information Operations School.

6. Ibid.

7. Air University, "Cyberspace & Information Operations Study Center," April 25, 2011, accessed June 2, 2011, www.au.af.mil/info-ops.

8. Kevin Maney, "If U.S. Launches Cyberattack, It Could Change Nature of War," *USA Today,* February 12, 2003, 3B.

9. SiliconIndia, "Terrorists' New Target: Hire Unemployed Techies," SiliconIndia News, January 10, 2010, accessed June 3, 2011, www.siliconindia.com/show news/Terrorists_new_target_Hire_unemployed_techies_-nid-64463.html.

10. Anthony Johnson and Kathy Hannon, "Terrorism Cyber Jihad," *The Advertiser* (Australia), May 24, 2008, Magazine 4.

11. Aaron Mannes and James Hendler, "The First Modern Cyberwar?," *Guardian*, August 22, 2008, accessed June 3, 2011, www.guardian.co.uk/commentis free/2008/aug/22/russia.georgia1.

12. "Russia: Still Second Rate And Unloved," StrategyWorld.com, August 20, 2008, accessed July 18, 2011, www.strategypage.com/qnd/russia/articles/20080820.aspx.

13. "Cyber-locked Georgia," The Confidential Resource, August 11, 2008, accessed June 3, 2011, www.confidentialresource.com/category/uncategorized.

14. Ministry of Foreign Affairs of Georgia, August 29, 2008, accessed June 3, 2011, georgiamfa.blogspot.com/2008_08_01_archive.html.

15. John Leyden, "Russian Spy Agencies Linked to Georgian Cyber-attacks," The Register, March 23, 2009, accessed June 3, 2011, www.theregister.co.uk/2009/03/23/georgia_russia_cyberwar_analysis.

16. "War, Redefined," *Los Angeles Times*, August 17, 2008, accessed June 3, 2011, www.latimes.com/news/opinion/la-ed-cyberwar17-2008aug17,0,5922456.story.

17. Christopher Rhoads, "Kyrgyzstan Knocked Offline," *Wall Street Journal,* January 28, 2009, A10.

18. Christopher Rhoads and Geoffrey A. Fowler, "Iran Pro-Regime Voices Multiply Online," *Wall Street Journal*, July 3, 2009, A7.

19. Siobhan Gorman and Evan Ramstad, "Cyber Blitz Hits U.S., Korea—Simple Attack on Government, Businesses Exposes Vulnerability; Pyongyang Suspected," *Wall Street Journal*, July 9, 2009, A1.

20. Maayana Miskin, "Report: IDF and Iran Engage in 'Cyber War'," Arutz Sheva, July 10, 2009, accessed June 3, 2011, www.israelnationalnews.com/News/ Flash.aspx/167783.

21. Elizabeth Arrott, "Iran: Computer Malware Attacked, Failed to Harm Nuclear Plant," Voice of America News, September 26, 2010, accessed June 3, 2011, www.voanews.com/english/news/Iran-Computer-Malware-Attacked-Failed-to- Harm-Nuclear-Plant-103819379.html.

22. Éanna Ó Caollai, "CAO to Carry Out Internal Inquiry Into Cyber Attack," *Irish Times*, August 24, 2010, 4.

23. "In the Battle of the Botnets Rustock Remains Dominant," Symantec Cloud, MessageLabs Intelligence, August 2010, accessed July 18, 2011, www.symantec cloud.com/en/in/globalthreats/overview/r_mli_reports. (Scroll to Message Labs Intelligence: August 2010.)

24. Iftikhar Alam, "Pakistan-India Cyber War Begins," *The Nation*, Pakistan, December 5, 2010, accessed June 2, 2011, www.nation.com.pk/pakistan-news- newspaper-daily-english-online/Politics/05-Dec-2010/PakistanIndia-cyber- war-begins.

25. D. A. Liptak, "WikiLeaks.org," Free Government Information, January 13, 2007, accessed June 2, 2011, freegovinfo.info/node/853.

26. Dean Wilson, "Anonymous Takes Down Visa, Amazon, PayPal, Swiss Bank, Assange prosecutor: Amazon and Facebook Next on Operation: Payback List," TechEYE.net, December 9, 2010, accessed June 2, 2011, www.techeye.net/ security/anonymous-takes-down-visa-amazon-paypal-swiss-bank-assange- prosecutor.

27. Jailan Zayan, "Egypt Activists Have Upper Hand in Cyber War," AFP, Feb 9, 2011, accessed June 2, 2011, www.google.com/hostednews/afp/article/ALeqM5gb Ox_PCgkBVkTJKfSYlr0wqPujoQ?docId=CNG.7ce7ae644708af2bfddba36e7 fd70750.141.

28. ColomboPage News Desk, "Sri Lanka Army Commander Says Cyber War Still Continues," ColomboPage, Sri Lanka, February 22, 2011, accessed June 2, 2011, www.colombopage.com/archive_11/Feb22_1298388902CH.php.

29. William Yong, "Government Of Iran Detects Cyberattack," *New York Times*, April 25, 2011, A12.

30. Robert McMillan, "Hackers Hit Scientology With Online Attack," IDG News, January 26, 2008, accessed July 18, 2011, www.pcworld.com/article/141839/ hackers_hit_scientology_with_online_attack.html.

31. Finlay Lewis, "Hacking Hunter," SignOnSanDiego.com, October 2, 2007, accessed June 3, 2011, weblog.signonsandiego.com/news/breaking/2007/10/hacking_hunter.html.

32. "Pentagon Reacts to Cyberattack," *Network World,* June 25, 2007, 4.

33. George W. Dinolt, Cynthia E. Irvine, and Timothy E. Levin, "Summary: Emergency Response for Cyber Infrastructure Management," Naval Postgraduate School, 2003, accessed June 3, 2011, www.hsdl.org/homesec/docs/dhs/nps10-072904-07.pdf.

34. U.S. Department of Transportation, Research and Special Programs Administration, "Final Report DOT-VNTSC-FHWA-04-02, Effects of Catastrophic Events on Transportation System Management and Operations: August 2003 Northeast Blackout, Great Lakes Region," May 2004, accessed July 18, 2011, ntl.bts.gov/lib/jpodocs/repts_te/14021_files/14021.pdf.

35. Barak Obama, "President-elect Speaks on the Need for Urgent Action on an American Recovery and Reinvestment Plan," Change.gov, January 8, 2010, accessed June 3, 2011, change.gov/newsroom/entry/president-elect_obama_speaks_on_the_need_for_urgent_action_on_an_american_r.

36. U.S. Department of Energy and The North American Electric Reliability Corporation, "High-Impact, Low-Frequency Event Risk to the North American Bulk Power System," June 2010, accessed June 3, 2011, www.nerc.com/files/HILF.pdf.

37. John Markoff, "Internet's Anonymity Makes Cyberattack Hard to Trace," *New York Times,* July 16, 2009, A5, accessed June 3, 2011, www.nytimes.com/2009/07/17/technology/17cyber.html.

38. U.S. Senate Committee on Governmental Affairs, "Unclassified Testimony for George J. Tenet, Director of Central Intelligence," June 24, 1998, accessed June 3, 2011, hsgac.senate.gov/62498dci.htm.

39. Dan Verton, "Experts Predict Major Cyberattack Coming," *Computerworld,* July 8, 2002, 8.

40. Jon Swartz, "Hackers Hijack Federal Computers," *USA Today,* August 30, 2004, B1.

41. Maney, 3B.

42. Bruce Schneier, "Counterpane: Attack Trends 2004 and 2005," *Queue,* June 2005, 52–53.

43. Crawford, "Information Warfare."

44. AT&T, "Business Continuity Study Results January–May 2006," accessed June 3, 2011, www.att.com/Common/files/pdf/biz_cont_full_report.pdf.

45. AT&T, "Business Continuity Survey 2008," accessed June 3, 2011, www.att.com/Common/merger/files/pdf/business_continuity_08/US_Survey_Results.pdf.

46. U.S. Government Accountability Office, "TECHNOLOGY ASSESSMENT Cybersecurity for Critical Infrastructure Protection," May 2004, accessed June 3, 2011, www.gao.gov/new.items/d04321.pdf.

47. U.S. Government Accountability Office, "INTERNET INFRASTRUCTURE DHS Faces Challenges in Developing a Joint Public/Private Recovery Plan," June 2006, accessed June 3, 2011, www.gao.gov/new.items/d06672.pdf.

48. U.S. Government Accountability Office, "CRITICAL INFRASTRUCTURE PROTECTION Multiple Efforts to Secure Control Systems Are Under Way, But Challenges Remain," September 2007, accessed June 3, 2011, www.gao.gov/new.items/d071036.pdf.

49. U.S. Government Accountability Office, "CRITICAL INFRASTRUCTURE PROTECTION DHS Needs to Better Address Its Cybersecurity Responsibilities," September 16, 2008, accessed June 3, 2011, www.gao.gov/new.items/d081157t.pdf.

50. Mark Loos, "Implementing a Local Security Program," SANS Institute, 2002, accessed June 3, 2011, www.sans.org/reading_room/whitepapers/warfare/implementing-local-security-program-protect-national-infrastructure-system-companies-facil_822.

51. Shannon N. Lawson, "Information Warfare: An Analysis of the Threat of Cyberterrorism Toward the US Critical Infrastructure," SANS Institute, 2003, accessed June 3, 2011, www.sans.org/reading_room/whitepapers/warfare/information-warfare-analysis-threat-cyberterrorism-critical-infrastruc_821.

52. Philip S. Antón, et al., "Finding and Fixing Vulnerabilities in Information Systems: The Vulnerability Assessment and Mitigation Methodology," RAND Corporation, 2003, accessed June 3, 2011, www.rand.org/pubs/monograph_reports/2005/MR1601.pdf.

53. Teresa Riordan, "An Architecture of Defense, and Offense to Protect Against Hackers," *New York Times,* August 5, 2002, C4.

54. Deborah Radcliff, "Should You Strike Back?" *Computerworld,* November 13, 2000, 73.

55. Michael Martinez, "Traditional Communications Systems Reliable in Disasters," GovExec.com, December 12, 2005, accessed June 3, 2011, www.govexec.com/ dailyfed/1205/121205tdpm1.htm.

56. Paul Piper and Miguel Ramos, "A Failure to Communicate: Politics, Scams, and Information Flow During Hurricane Katrina," *Searcher,* June 2006, 40.

57. Edward E. Balkovich and Robert H. Anderson, "Critical Infrastructures Will Remain Vulnerable: Neighbourhoods Must Fend for Themselves," *Journal of Critical Infrastructures,* 2004, 8.

58. Piper, 40.

59. Balkovich, 8.

60. Piper, 40.

CHAPTER 6

The Intentional Misleading
of the American Public:

Political Misinformation

Laura Gordon-Murnane

"Misleading the public is a bipartisan habit."
—AP Washington bureau chief
Ron Fournier, May 19, 2010[1]

"It ain't what you don't know that gets you into trouble. It's what you know for sure that just ain't so."
—Attributed to Mark Twain

Twenty-first-century American journalists believe that by educating and informing the public, they enable citizens to engage in civil debate concerning issues of national importance, choose the best and brightest to lead the country, and come to appropriate conclusions on the actions needed to solve the nation's economic, social, energy, and environmental problems.[2]

If only it were true.

Political misinformation is alive and well on the internet, where a large percentage of Americans now get their news.[3] People who wish to inject intentionally false rumors, deceptions, and other inaccuracies into the mainstream press can do so virally by taking advantage of the demands of the 24/7 news cycle. In addition to its own reporting, the traditional media's news stream is fueled by blogs, social networks, Twitter, YouTube, stories from news aggregators such as Google News, and the mobile web. While much of what these sources offer is legitimate and factually correct, there is also rumor, innuendo, and gossip without any factual basis at all. Once in the mainstream, this misinformation receives additional visibility and credibility. Because it remains mostly unchecked along the way, it is readily accepted as legitimate news and becomes difficult to correct.

It sometimes seems as if many Americans are merely uninformed when, in fact, they may have been intentionally *mis*informed. This problem presents a considerable barrier to thoughtful decision making by government leaders and ordinary citizens.[4]

The "Birther" Rumor

The "birther" rumor is a well-known example of intentional misinformation in the political arena. The United States Constitution requires that the president be a natural-born citizen. President Barack Obama was born in Hawaii on August 4, 1961, and during the 2008 presidential campaign he released a scanned image of his birth certificate. Hawaii's heath director and the Hawaii register of statistics have confirmed the validity of the birth certificate.

That hasn't stopped the "birther" movement and its claim that President Obama was born outside the U.S. It is not clear where this claim began, but somehow it took hold in the imagination of many citizens of the U.S., who now question the legitimacy of the Obama presidency. A 2010 ABC News/Washington Post poll reported that about 20 percent of Americans believed that he was born outside the U.S.; 31 percent of Republicans, Tea Party members, evangelical white Protestants, and supporters of John McCain believed the same. In his own party, 15 percent of Democrats and 12 percent of liberals believed that he was born outside the U.S.[5] A month earlier, the *New York Times* and CBS News had released a poll (April 4–12, 2010) that found that only 58 percent of the public and 41 percent of the Tea Party believed that the president was born in the U.S. Thirty-two percent of Republicans believed that the president was born in another country.[6] FactCheck.org, among others, has debunked the false rumors of Obama's birth residence, but the intentional misinformation persisted into 2011.[7]

The "birther" issue captured headlines 3 years after Barack Obama was elected president when real estate mogul Donald Trump jumped on the "birther" bandwagon in his hinted-at campaign for president in 2012.[8] FactCheck.org provides a thorough and compelling analysis of Trump's concerns and claims (www.fact check.org/2011/04/donald-youre-fired).[9] More than a handful of state legislatures contributed to the "birther" issue by introducing legislation that "would require future presidential candidates to document their eligibility with birth certificates or other forms of proof that they were born in the United States."[10] And the state legislature of Arizona became the first in the nation to pass a bill requiring presidential candidates "to provide proof of citizenship in order to get on the state's ballot."[11]

In April 2011, President Obama's lawyers requested a waiver of state policy from the Hawaii State Department of Health to release the long form of his birth certificate in order to put this issue to rest.[12]

How Intentional Political Misinformation Is Spread

The "birther" rumor is just one example of how intentional political misinformation spreads more rapidly than ever. There are four realities we face when dealing with this phenomenon, realities that pose a challenge to a democratic society based on an informed citizenry:

- The decline of trust in government and the intense political polarization of the population have contributed to the spread of intentionally false rumors and misinformation. This misinformation often comes in the way the issues are framed.

- Once intentionally false rumors have been released into the wild, it is almost impossible to correct them.

- The mainstream press plays a role in the spread of misinformation and rumors.

- There are high costs to such political misinformation.

After exploring these realities, we will present the options and tools that are available to assist in identifying intentionally false rumors and provide ways to temper and mitigate their costs.

Distrust of Government

The public's trust of government is at its lowest point ever. A survey published in March 2011 by the Pew Research Center for the People & the Press "finds a modest recovery in public trust in government from historic lows last year. Yet even with this uptick, the general mood remains overwhelmingly negative. Just 29% say they can trust the government in Washington to do what is right just about always or most of the time, up from 22% last March. About seven-in-ten (69%) say they trust the government only some of the time or never, compared with 76% a year ago."[13] As in a previous survey, the American public "continues to express negative views of Congress, as well as Republican and Democratic congressional leaders. Just 34% say they have a favorable opinion of Congress, up slightly from 26% a year ago; a majority (57%) has an unfavorable view. Comparable percentages say they approve of the job performance of Republican (36%) and Democratic (33%) congressional leaders."[14]

President Obama, in his 2009 State of the Union address, called this a "deficit of trust, deep and corrosive doubts about how Washington works. … Washington may think that saying anything about the other side, no matter how false, no matter how malicious, is just part of the game. But it's precisely such politics that has stopped either party from helping the American people. Worse yet, it's sowing further division among our citizens, further distrust in our government."[15] Partisan gridlock stymies policy agendas and leaves Americans believing that Congress cannot get anything done and cannot deliver meaningful solutions to help the nation's ills.

However, Obama's words have had little to no effect. The *National Journal* reported in its Annual Congressional Vote Ratings for 2009 that "the past year in Congress was defined by liberal–conservative battles over economic issues, with health care reform dominating the debate and demonstrating the philosophical chasm between the two parties on the role of government in the nation's commerce."[16] The partisan divide that threatens Washington has created a fertile environment for people on both sides to distrust each other and to accept the false statements and distortions on just about everything people on the other side propose, say, endorse, and support. University of Michigan political scientist Brendan Nyhan reports that as American politics have become more polarized and divided, "legislators, pundits, and interest groups have waged a vicious communications war against each other, making misleading claims about the other side and its policy agenda."[17] Given this behavior, it is not surprising that the American public distrusts its political leaders.

Every major political issue, whether climate change, lobbying reform, or immigration reform, is shaped and defined by its own language—the terms, phrases, titles, memes, metaphors, and messages—that captures its meaning and becomes a shorthand way to describe a complex issue. To really own an issue requires that politicians own the language associated with that issue. If one can capture how Americans read, hear, and share the debate surrounding any important political issue, then one "owns" the issue and can offer legislative solutions that address or evade the problems facing the country. The group, party, or organization that can frame the issue to its advantage can affect how the American public will use these frames to make sense of the policy debates and can fuse the frames with their own experiences, their values, beliefs, and political ideology. "Audiences rely on frames to make sense of and discuss an issue; journalists use frames to craft interesting and appealing news reports; policymakers apply frames to define policy options and reach decisions; and experts employ frames to simplify technical details and make them persuasive."[18] If you can frame it, you can claim it.

A good example is the debate over climate change that has polarized the American public for more than 20 years. Formerly referred to as *global warming*, the language used to define the issue has been changed to reflect the possibility that the issue has more to do with climate change than whether the entire Earth is warming. Both Republicans and Democrats have employed their own set of frames to capture the issue and have used trusted spokesmen and organizations to make their positions accessible to American citizens.

Republicans have used think tanks, conservative commentators, and politicians to develop talk points, white papers, and speeches that challenge the scientific evidence of climate change by framing it as "scientific uncertainty" and questioning "whether human activities drive climate change while also arguing that any action to curb it will lead to dire economic consequences."[19]

The conservative strategy has also used the press to disseminate misleading or inaccurate information about climate change. "As political reporters applied their preferred *conflict and strategy* frame to the policy debate—focusing on which side was winning, the personalities involved, and their message strategies—they also engaged in the same type of false balance that has been common to coverage of elections and issues. In other words, by giving equal weight to contrarian views on climate science, journalists presented the false impression that there was limited expert agreement on the causes of climate change."[20]

James Inhofe, Republican senator from Oklahoma, is one of the strongest and loudest voices claiming that the Earth's climate is not changing because of human activity. He uses the power of his Senate office to challenge the scientific basis for climate change and purposely uses "the fragmented news media, with appearances at television outlets ... on political talk radio, and web traffic driven to his blog from the Drudge Report" to amplify his position that climate change is not manmade but due to natural causes.[21]

Conservative commentators and columnists such as George Will, Charles Krauthammer, and Tony Blankley use their media voices to give credibility and support to the frames of scientific uncertainty and dire economic consequences that are advocated by the Republican Party.

The Democrats have used their own star, former vice president Al Gore, author of the book and Emmy-award-winning documentary *An Inconvenient Truth*, to gain hold of the climate change debate and move it away from the "scientific and economic uncertainty" frame by emphasizing the threat of a looming "climate crisis." If we don't act soon, we will suffer from terrible hurricanes, "polar bears perched precariously on shrinking ice floes, scorched, drought-stricken earth, blazing wild fires, or famous cities or landmarks under water due to future sea-level rise."[22]

Another tactic recently employed by environmentalists is to counter the dire economic consequences frame with one "in favor of action, recasting climate change as an opportunity to grow the economy." Think clean energy, green jobs, green technology, and sustainable economic prosperity. The goal of this framing strategy is to "catalyze a more diverse social movement—perhaps even engaging support for energy policies among Republicans, who think predominantly in terms of market opportunities, or labor advocates, who value the possibility of job growth."[23]

Public health officials are also trying to frame climate change as a public health issue. In this frame, the consequences of climate change are tied to the increasing problems of disease: asthma, allergies, and the spread of infectious diseases that hit at-risk populations including the elderly and the young. The news coverage no longer focuses on stranded polar bears and melting glaciers. It takes the issue to a more personal and meaningful level: your health and the health of your family, neighborhood, and community.

Dealing with the issues involving climate change requires political risk taking, leadership, and a strong will. It remains to be seen who will successfully craft a message, capture the hearts and minds of the American public, and offer solutions that address all the implications of climate change. What we read online as fact is not always based in fact; at times it is intentionally misleading the reader to a point of view not based on scientific evidence. This is how framing an issue and how the use of the internet makes a difference in spreading the "facts."

Correcting Political Misinformation

When it comes to American politics, it is sometimes hard to know what is true and what is false, and according to whom. Once a piece of information is released, citizens and voters have to process the information and come to some conclusion about a political leader, a legislative solution, or a regulatory plan. If the information is distorted and inaccurate to begin with, or gets mangled by the media, people will be basing their decisions on faulty information; it becomes much harder to dislodge the incorrect information and replace it with the correct version.

Political scientists James H. Kuklinski and Brendan Nyhan have conducted research on political misinformation and how well citizens deal with information that challenges, contradicts, or outright shows their beliefs to be incorrect. They asked if citizens use corrective information to update their beliefs, modify their positions to reflect the new information, and adapt to alternative political solutions to problems. Their results in short: "Citizens tend to resist facts."[24] Psychologists have studied this phenomenon and found that people will try to avoid psychological conflict, which is also called cognitive dissonance. When people are faced with a problem, they tend to seek information that confirms their beliefs and avoid information that is inconsistent with those views. According to Nyhan, they are also likely to "process information with a bias toward their pre-existing views, disparaging contradictory information while uncritically accepting information that is consistent with their beliefs." The bottom line is that "exposure to and acceptance of politically salient misperceptions will frequently divide along partisan or ideological lines."[25] In other words, we look for evidence that supports our point of view, and we figure out mental shortcuts that help us disregard and discredit information that does not support our point of view. Psychologists call this "confirmation bias," and it not only "colors how we see things, but how we reason, as well."[26]

Consequently, Democrats or Republicans, liberals or conservatives, Independents or Tea Party members could all have the same pool of facts but interpret them in ways that justify their opinions or party platforms. Research conducted by Stony Brook University political scientists Charles Taber and Milton Lodge found that "strong partisans ... make every effort to maintain their existing opinions by seeking out confirming evidence, counterarguing information that does not fit their preexisting conceptions, and attributing more strength to arguments that match their opinions." Partisans will engage in "mental gymnastics" and "instead of promoting learning, provide skills in resisting unwanted information."[27] Brooks Jackson and Kathleen Hall Jamieson write that "content that agrees with our own views simply seems true and [is] thus not very noteworthy, while material that counters our biases stands out in our minds and makes us look for a reason to reject it. So to a conservative, news with a conservative slant is fair; to a liberal, news with a liberal slant is fair; and to both, there is something unfair somewhere in any news program that tries to balance alternative points of view."[28]

Kuklinski has found that when it comes to the facts, people hold inaccurate factual beliefs and do so confidently; they use this incorrect information to form preferences. Furthermore, "not only does this misinformation function as a barrier to factually educating citizens, it can lead to collective preferences that differ significantly from those that would exist if people were adequately informed."[29] In other words, the more misinformed we are, the more convinced we are that the beliefs we hold are correct, and the more we are in danger of supporting poor policy decisions.

Nyhan asks if misinformation, false information, or unsubstantiated beliefs about political issues can be corrected. In his research, he found that factual corrections failed to reduce misperceptions among ideological groups. He also found that direct factual corrections, instead of changing minds, actually had the opposite effect—a "backfire effect"—whereby partisans held on to their original positions even more strongly, even in the face of direct evidence that contradicted their beliefs.[30] He reported on experiments that tested the beliefs of both Republicans and Democrats with regard to their beliefs/views about the Iraq War and the existence of weapons of mass destruction. One of the key arguments for going to war against Iraq was the belief that Saddam Hussein's government possessed biological and chemical weapons. Subjects were asked to read a "mock news article" that reported on a Bush campaign stop in Pennsylvania where the president gave a strong defense of the Iraq War. The mock news story quotes a line from a speech President Bush actually gave at a campaign stop in Wilkes-Barre, Pennsylvania: "There was a risk, a real risk, that Saddam Hussein would pass weapons or materials or information to terrorist networks, and in the world after September 11th, that was a risk we could not afford to take."

The subjects were then asked to read the Duelfer Report, the final report issued by the Iraq Survey Group that had been tasked to find out if Iraq actually had weapons of mass destruction before the U.S. invasion of Iraq in 2003. The Duelfer Report "documents the lack of Iraqi WMD stockpiles or an active production program immediately prior to the US invasion." After reading the article and the report, subjects were asked whether they agreed with the following statement: "Immediately before the U.S. invasion, Iraq had [an] active weapons of mass destruction program, the ability to produce these weapons, and large stockpiles of WMD, but Saddam Hussein was able to hide or destroy these weapons right before the U.S. forces arrived." Subjects responded to the statement on a 5-point scale ranging from "strongly agree" (1) to "strongly disagree" (5).[31]

What effect did the Duelfer Report have on correcting the original statement by President Bush that Iraq could give weapons of mass destruction to terrorists? The answer is that it depended on the political ideology of the participant. "Liberals shifted in the direction of even greater disagreement with the statement."[32] However, those who identified themselves as conservatives moved in the opposite direction: They agreed with the statement. For Republicans, the new information challenged their core beliefs about the reasons for going to war, and it challenged their belief in President Bush and his administration.

Cognitive dissonance reared its head. "In other words, the correction backfired. Conservatives who received a correction telling them that Iraq did not have WMD were more likely to believe that Iraq had WMD."[33] Cass Sunstein, the administrator of the Office of Information and Regulatory Affairs in the Obama administration and author of *On Rumors: How Falsehoods Spread, Why We Believe Them, What Can Be Done*, comments, "Not only did the correction fail, but it also had a polarizing effect; it divided people more sharply than they had been divided before."[34] Although these findings challenge the effectiveness of corrections, the mainstream media, non-profits, and the political blogosphere passionately believe that for the sustainability and survivability of democracy, political leaders must be held accountable for what they say and do. Armed with this belief, the mainstream news media has enthusiastically championed a renewed interest in fact-checking the statements, campaign ads, blog posts, Twitter feeds, Facebook updates, and Sunday morning interviews of political leaders, pundits, and the talking heads on radio, television, and the internet.

The Role of the Media in Spreading Intentional Misinformation

What role do the news media play in the spread of intentional political misinformation? Over the last decade, the news industry as a whole and the newspaper industry in particular have been under a triple assault: The rise of digital technology, the decline in profitability through the decline in advertising and classified ads, and a decline in readership have all brought the news media into crisis mode.[35] This crisis threatens the sustainability and viability of what Alex Jones, Pulitzer Prize-winning journalist and director of the Joan Shorenstein Center on the Press, Politics and Public Policy at Harvard's John F. Kennedy School of Government, calls "accountability news," that is, the news that holds government and those in power accountable. Traditional journalists believe that "fact-based accountability news is the essential food supply of democracy and that without enough of this health nourishment, democracy will weaken, sicken, or even fail."[36] For a long time, this type of news "has been somewhat sheltered by an economic model that was able to provide extra resources beyond what readers and advertisers would financially support. This kind of news is expensive to produce, especially investigative reporting."[37] Accountability news—the hardcore, investigative, in-depth journalism—costs a lot, not many people read it, and it is being replaced by "news of assertion" rather than by "news of verification."[38] This is a triple assault.

The news media face another serious problem: The American public no longer trusts and respects it. Rasmussen Reports, an American public opinion polling firm, conducted a telephone survey of likely U.S. voters in June 2010 and found that "sixty-six percent of U.S. voters describe themselves as at least somewhat angry at the media, including 33 percent who are angry."[39] In addition, according to Rasmussen, "68 percent say most reporters when covering a political campaign try to help the candidate they want to win" and "54 percent of voters think most reporters would hide any information they uncovered that might hurt a candidate they wanted to win, up seven points from November 2008." According to the Pew Project for Excellence in Journalism's 2009 annual State of the News Media report, "the public retained a deep skepticism about what they see, hear and read in the media. No major news outlet—broadcast or cable, print or online—stood out as particularly credible. There was no indication that Americans altered their fundamental judgment that the news media are politically biased, that stories are often inaccurate and that journalists do not care about the people they report on."[40] Jones commented that "traditional news organizations have lost part of their ability to persuade people with facts. Unwelcome facts are almost as easy to dismiss these days as unwelcome opinions. ... And the reason that losing the news—the accountability news—is so important is that a dearth of reliable information will force us to chart our national path with pseudo news and opinion that may be more appealing but will be far less reliable. ... When the news media are doing their job, we have enough information to make informed decisions, and when they do not, we are—as a nation—in jeopardy of being misled."[41]

The financial pressures facing the news media and the decline in investigative journalism have also allowed the spread of lazy journalism, comfortable journalism. In a panel discussion at the 2010 Personal Democracy Forum in New York, Bill Adair, editor of PolitiFact.com and the Washington bureau chief for the *St. Petersburg Times*, revealed that when he looked back at his reporting during the 2004 presidential campaign, he felt guilty that he had let the candidates get away with "exaggerations and falsehoods." According to Adair, the media did not do more fact-checking and accountability news because presidential campaign coverage had become all about the horse race. It became very easy and comfortable to report on who's up and who's down in the polls. The campaign was reported as if these statistics were the most important ones to cover. It was comfortable journalism. This led him to create PolitiFact.com, a means of fact-checking the comments, statements, and political campaign ads of presidential candidates, congressmen and senators, cabinet officers, and political pundits and talk show hosts.[42] Accountability journalism began to make a comeback.

It is commonly thought that the media are supposed to be neutral and objective in their reporting and presentation of facts. Jones defines journalistic objectivity as "a genuine effort to be an honest broker when it comes to news. That means playing it straight without favoring one side when the facts are in dispute, regardless of your own views and preferences." It also means "not trying to create the illusion of fairness by letting advocates pretend in your journalism that there is a debate about the facts when the weight of truth is clear. He-said/she-said reporting, which just pits one voice against another, has become the discredited face of objectivity."[43]

Media contribution to intentional political misinformation can be seen in the coverage of the climate change issue. Marc Ambinder, politics editor for *The Atlantic,* wrote in a blog post on the TheAtlantic.com:

> I won't pretend that climate change isn't happening, and that the scientific consensus, which grows more solid by the day (and not less solid), holds that humans are responsible

for much of this change. We can validly debate the solutions, but it is simply stupid to pretend, for the sake of appearing to be fair, as if there is a fundamental scientific debate that has yet to be solved. On the other side of the coin, simply acknowledging the science does not presuppose any particular solution. You *can* cover a debate about how to fix global warming, and whether the trade-offs that must be made are worth their price. These are open, contestable questions. The fact of global warming isn't. [44]

He-said/she-said journalism only intensifies the political polarization in Washington. Jay Rosen, professor of journalism at New York University, complained about the failure of the Sunday morning talk shows as examples of this type of journalism. These shows only exacerbate the political divide and division of Washington: "Inviting partisans on television to polarize us some more would seem to be an obvious loser, especially because the limited airtime compresses political speech and guarantees a struggle for the microphone." The entire Sunday morning news show is an invitation for politicians to "evade, deny, elide, demagogue and confuse. ..."[45] Do these shows really add new information, new understanding, and careful, rigorous thought and analysis for their audience? When the show is over, do you feel better educated about the issues of the day? Rosen answers this with a resounding no. "This pattern tends to strand viewers in the senseless middle. We either don't know whom to believe, and feel helpless. Or we curse both sides for their distortions. Or we know enough to know who is bullshitting us more and wonder why the host doesn't." Rosen offers a solution: "Fact-check what your guests say on Sunday and run it online Wednesday. ... Whoever was bullshitting us more could expect to hear about it from *Meet the Press* staff on Wednesday."[46] Presumably, those politicians whose statements were less than truthful would be more careful in what they say or would not be asked back to the show. *Meet the Press* has declined to act on this suggestion, but Jake Tapper, interim host of ABC News's *This Week*, decided to work with PolitiFact.com to do exactly what Rosen proposed. CNN's *Reliable Sources*, hosted by Howard Kurtz, and *The Rachel Maddow Show* have regular fact-checking segments as well.

The news media in general and newspapers in particular have served an important watchdog function, making sure that our government and political leaders are held accountable for the things they say and do. With the financial instability of newspapers, the watchdog and investigative reporting services have suffered greatly. Washington news bureaus have cut their staffs, and far fewer reporters are covering the "many federal departments, agencies or bureaus that are not part of the daily news cycle."[47] Many federal departments issuing federal regulations that affect everything from the food we eat to the water we drink to the air we breathe are "uncovered or undercovered by the mainstream media." If not for newspapers, the nation as a whole would not have known about "the Pentagon Papers, Watergate, Iran-Contra, Jack Abramoff, campaign finance. … Now that so many newspapers have forsaken the capital, it should not be surprising that the quality of reporting on the federal government has slipped. The watchdogs have abandoned their posts."[48] Nonprofit organizations such as ProPublica and bloggers and citizen journalists are filling in the gaps and fulfilling the oversight and accountability roles that the mainstream press previously served. But the jury is still out on how long they can continue to afford to do this. Even so, it would not let the mainstream media off the hook; they bear some responsibility for their choices in what to cover and how much space to devote to any specific issue.

The Costs of Intentional Political Misinformation

What are the costs of political misinformation? In the hyperconnected world of the internet (and because it is hard to remove something once it has made it onto the internet), the rumors, falsehoods, innuendo, and half-truths become almost impossible to debunk or dispel. Rumors "cast doubt on their subjects' honesty, decency, fairness, patriotism, and sometimes sanity," and the internet allows these rumors to spread with devastating speed and efficiency.[49] The intentional spread of a false statement about the insolvency of a particular financial institution on Wall Street can send the stock market plummeting, causing real financial hardship and global turmoil. Political issues of national importance are subject to rumors and distortions that tap into the fears, anger, and emotions of the population. Distortions of public policies are designed to discredit not only the policy initiative but the political leadership that is offering legislative solutions to national problems. The derailment of policy debates due to misinformation creates delays in programs; this results in postponed projects that eventually carry a greater financial cost. The economic costs can be steep.

Rumors and lies find acceptance and sustainability, depending on the convictions, beliefs, and prior knowledge of citizens. If you hear a rumor about a politician whom you dislike, you are more inclined to believe the rumor than if it concerned a political leader whom you feel shares your values and beliefs. During the 2008 presidential campaign, it was rumored that vice presidential candidate Sarah Palin thought "Africa was a country rather than a continent, because that ridiculous confusion fit with what they already thought about Governor Palin."[50] Likewise, other groups believed during the campaign that Barack Obama is a Muslim, that he was born outside the U.S., and that he "pals around with terrorists."[51] Intentional misinformation such as this can cost a candidate an election and possibly cause a change in the balance of power in Washington.

Tactics for Fighting Political Misinformation

The internet can work both to spread rumors and to quash them. During the 2008 presidential election, the Obama campaign launched the website FightTheSmears.com to identify and debunk the false rumors. "Once false rumors about then-Senator Obama were explicitly framed as 'smears,' they could and would be deemed unreliable." The rumors identified as smears were therefore considered just that and not worth believing.[52]

One tactic that voters can take to combat misinformation is to demand that political leaders respect the facts, and if they don't, hold them accountable. The vast resources and tools on the web can help voters identify political misinformation and hold political leaders accountable for what they say and do, and voters can then take appropriate action in the voting booth.

Roughly, the tools are organized into six categories: fact-checking tools, bias in media sites, media organizations watching the media sites, political blogs, accountability and transparency organizations, and government sites.

Fact-Checking Tools

Greg Sargent wrote in his Plum Line blog in May 2010, "Who woulda thunk it: Fact-checking is popular!"[53] Newspapers, watchdog organizations, and political bloggers are beginning to offer corrections and thoughtful analysis of statements, positions, campaign ads, and policy debates. The following are some of the resources they use.

PolitiFact.com
www.politifact.com
   PolitiFact.com is a project of the *St. Petersburg Times*. The site examines the statements of the president, cabinet secretaries, congressmen and senators, lobbyists, and political pundits. It rates the accuracy of statements by using the Truth-O-Meter, a six-point rating system (True, Mostly True, Half True, Barely True, False, and Pants on Fire) that looks at a politician's original statement in its full context. PolitiFact.com tries to locate the original source of the statement and combines that with original government reports and interviews with impartial experts, and then provides a final rating. PolitiFact.com provides a complete bibliography of the sources used for each analysis.

   The *St. Petersburg Times* is also working with news organizations nationwide to provide the same tools for state politics. This list includes some of the most well-known partnerships between PolitiFact.com and the news organizations that monitor the assertions of politicians:

- PolitiFact Florida (www.politifact.com/florida) is a partnership of the *St. Petersburg Times* and *Miami Herald*.

- PolitiFact Georgia (www.politifact.com/georgia) is a partnership of the *Atlanta Journal-Constitution* and PolitiFact.com.

- PolitiFact Ohio (www.politifact.com/ohio) is a partnership of the *Cleveland Plain Dealer* and PolitiFact.com.

- PolitiFact Oregon (www.politifact.com/oregon) is a partnership of *The Oregonian*, OregonLive.com, and PolitiFact.com.

- PolitiFact Rhode Island (www.politifact.com/rhode-island) is a partnership of the *Providence Journal* and PolitiFact.com.

- PolitiFact Texas (www.politifact.com/texas) is a partnership of the *Austin American-Statesman* and PolitiFact.com.

- PolitiFact Virginia (www.politifact.com/virginia) is a partnership of the *Richmond Times Dispatch* and PolitiFact.com.

- PolitiFact Wisconsin (www.politifact.com/wisconsin) is a partnership of the *Journal Sentinel*, JSonline.com, and PolitiFact.com.

FactCheck.org

www.factcheck.org

FactCheck.org is a project of the Annenberg Public Policy Center of the University of Pennsylvania. It monitors "the factual accuracy of what is said by major U.S. political players in the form of TV ads, debates, speeches, interviews and news releases."[54] It provides a detailed analysis of political statements and a list of sources to back up its conclusions. The site also provides FactCheck Radio, FactCheck Wire, and Ask FactCheck.

PoliGraph

minnesota.publicradio.org/collections/special/columns/polinaut/archive/poligraph

PoliGraph, a fact-checking feature launched by Minnesota Public Radio News and the Humphrey Institute of Public Affairs at the University of Minnesota, looks at political spin in Minnesota politics. PoliGraph, published weekly, takes an in-depth look at political claims made by members of the three major parties in the state and checks them against neutral sources for accuracy.

Meet the Facts

www.meetthefacts.com

Meet the Facts is a nonpartisan, grassroots effort inspired by Professor Jay Rosen's suggestion to fact-check the Sunday morning talk shows. David Gregory, the host of *Meet the Press*, has declined Rosen's suggestion, arguing that the people who watch the show can do their own fact-checking. Students Paul Breer and Chas Danner have launched Meet the Facts to fact-check the comments made on *Meet the Press* and publish their analysis several days after the broadcast.

Bias in Media Sites

These organizations evaluate bias in media coverage of politics.

Accuracy in Media

www.aim.org

Accuracy in Media is a nonprofit, grassroots citizens' organization that reports on liberal media bias.

Fairness & Accuracy in Reporting (FAIR)

www.fair.org

FAIR, launched in 1986, is a national media watch group that reports on conservative media bias.

Center for Media and Democracy

www.prwatch.org

The Center for Media and Democracy, founded in 1993, is an independent, nonprofit, nonpartisan public interest organization that focuses on investigating and countering spin (coming from corporations, industries, and government agencies) that affects our health, liberty, security, economic opportunities, environment, and the vitality of the democratic process. The center publishes PRWatch, SourceWatch, and BanksterUSA.

Media Matters for America

www.mediamatters.org

Media Matters for America, founded in 2004, is a web-based, nonprofit, progressive research and information center that monitors, analyzes, and seeks to correct conservative misinformation in the U.S. media.

Organization of News Ombudsmen

newsombudsmen.org

The Organization of News Ombudsmen provides a useful list of domestic and international newspapers and news media that have an ombudsman—a staff member who handles complaints and who attempts to find mutually satisfactory solutions.

Media Organizations Watching the Media Sites

The following sites are watchdogs that watch the watchdogs, based on the principle that it is always good to know what's going on in your own house. The sites selected are not afraid to criticize the media when they think they are wrong.

On the Media

www.onthemedia.org

On the Media examines how the news is made and "casts an incisive eye on fluctuations in the marketplace of ideas, and examines threats to the freedom of information and expression in America and abroad." Hosts Bob Garfield and Brooke Gladstone are willing to challenge any guest who seems to play loose with the facts.

The Pew Research Center for the People & the Press

www.people-press.org

The Pew Research Center for the People & the Press is an independent, nonpartisan public opinion research organization that studies attitudes toward politics, the press, and public policy issues. In this role, it serves as a valuable information resource for political leaders, journalists, scholars, and citizens.

Regret the Error

www.regrettheerror.com

Regret the Error reports on media corrections, retractions, apologies, clarifications, and trends regarding accuracy and honesty in the press. The site was launched in 2004 by Craig Silverman, currently the managing editor for PBS's MediaShift. Silverman also writes a weekly column of the same name on accuracy and errors for the *Columbia Journalism Review* (www.cjr.org/regret_the_error).

Political Blogs

The political blogosphere is a vibrant, messy marketplace of ideas, viewpoints, and characters. All sides have their blogging champions, and here is a short list that offers political diversity and thoughtful commentary.

RealClearPolitics

www.realclearpolitics.com

Founded in 2000 by Chicago-based bloggers John McIntyre and Tom Bevan, RealClearPolitics is a nonpartisan data aggregator for political news and polling data. The founders are self-described conservatives, but the site aims for ideological diversity.

Memeorandum

www.memeorandum.com

Memeorandum is a political news aggregator. It autogenerates a news summary every 5 minutes, drawing on experts and pundits, insiders and outsiders, media professionals, and amateur bloggers.

Talking Points Memo

www.talkingpointsmemo.com

Launched by Josh Marshall during the Florida vote recount in November 2000, this is the flagship blog of TPM Media LLC, which also publishes TPMMuckraker, TPMDC, TPMtv, and TPMCafe. The site specializes in original reporting on government and politics and offers breaking news coverage, investigative reporting, high-profile guest bloggers, and a book club.

InstaPundit

www.pajamasmedia.com/instapundit

InstaPundit is a political blog by Professor Glenn Reynolds of the University of Tennessee. His interests are wide-ranging, including domestic policy, technology, and foreign policy. He describes himself as a libertarian.

FiveThirtyEight

www.fivethirtyeight.com

FiveThirtyEight is a nonpartisan polling aggregation site created by Nate Silver. In August 2010, this site was relaunched under the *New York Times* domain.

Teagan Goddard's Political Wire

www.politicalwire.com

Teagan Goddard's Political Wire, which was launched in 1999, is one of the most important political sites on the web. Read by both Republicans and Democrats, the site provides a daily compilation of political polling news, links, and statements by political leaders.

techPresident

www.techpresident.com

techPresident was started by Andrew Rasiej and Micah L. Sifry as a cross-partisan group blog covering how the 2008 presidential candidates were using the internet, and vice versa, how content generated by voters affected the campaign. techPresident has since expanded its coverage to include "everything from how President Obama is using the web, to how campaigns at all levels are going online, to how voters are responding and creating their own user-generated content."[55]

Accountability and Transparency Organizations

Accountability and transparency have gained greater currency since the 2008 presidential election. Here is a mix of independent organizations dedicated to bringing accountability and transparency to American politics.

Center for Responsive Politics's OpenSecrets.org

www.opensecrets.org

The Center for Responsive Politics tracks the influence of money and lobbying in U.S. politics and its effect on elections and public policy. It maintains an extensive public online database of campaign fundraising data where you can find out which groups contribute to specific members of the House and Senate.

ProPublica

www.propublica.org

ProPublica, launched in June 2008, is an independent, nonprofit newsroom that produces investigative journalism in the public interest. ProPublica offers in-depth articles and a variety of web-based tools that allow citizens to watch what is going on in Washington.

Sunlight Foundation

www.sunlightfoundation.com

The Sunlight Foundation uses cutting-edge technology and ideas to make the government transparent and accountable. Check out some of the tools it has created including Transparency Data (www.transparencydata.com) or Sunlight Labs (www.sunlightlabs.com).

Government Sites

The federal government has set up the following websites that can help citizens track where federal tax dollars are being spent and which government information technology projects are working or not. It has also created a centralized website that makes available to the public data sets and data tools created and released by federal agencies.

USAspending.gov

www.usaspending.gov

USAspending.gov gives the public information about how their tax dollars are spent. Citizens can find out about the different types of contracts, grants, loans, and other types of spending the federal government offers. The site provides a broad picture of the federal spending processes.

Data.gov

www.data.gov

Launched in May 2009, Data.gov makes available machine-readable data sets created by the executive agencies of the federal government.

IT Dashboard

www.itdashboard.gov

The IT Dashboard provides the public with an online window into the details of federal information technology investments and provides users with the ability to track the progress of investments over time.

Tips on Identifying Political Misinformation

So, how do we spot the rumors, half-truths, and misinformation on political sites? As with the other subjects discussed in *Web of Deceit*, evaluate the sites' authors, points of view, and other factors found in Appendix A, "Evaluating Websites." Investigate the veracity of statistics used to bolster opinions. Sometimes dramatic photos tell only one side of a story, so investigate what else might have been going on. If there are vague phrases in place of straightforward language, find another source for this information that might be more specific. Try to determine the underlying mission of organizations sponsoring websites and advertisements (e.g., UnionFacts.com is not pro-union). Investigate the source of funding, read the "About Us" section, and get a second source to confirm important facts. And be sure to keep an open mind. You may be the one who's been misinformed.

Endnotes

1. Greg Sargent, "Who Woulda Thunk It: Fact-Checking Is Popular!" Plum Line, May 19, 2010, accessed June 6, 2011, voices.washingtonpost.com/plumline/2010/05/who_woulda_thunk_it_fact-check.html.

2. Herbert J. Gans, "News & the News Media in the Digital Age: Implications for Democracy," *Daedalus*, Spring 2010, accessed June 6, 2011, findarticles.com/p/articles/mi_qa3671/is_201004//ai_n53927247/?tag=content;col1.

3. Kristen Purcell, et al., "Understanding the Participatory News Consumer," Pew Internet & American Life Project, March 1, 2010, accessed June 6, 2011, www.pewinternet.com/Reports/2010/Online-News.aspx.

4. James H. Kuklinski, "The Limits of Facts in Citizen Decision-Making," *Extensions,* Fall 2007, 1, accessed June 6, 2011, www.ou.edu/carlalbertcenter/extensions/fall2007/Kuklinski.pdf.

5. ABC News/Washington Post Poll, "Half of 'Birthers' Call It 'Suspicion'; A Third Approve of Obama Anyway," May 9, 2010, accessed June 6, 2011, abcnews.go.com/images/PollingUnit/Birthers_new.pdf.

6. New York Times/CBS News Poll, "Poll: 'Birther' Myth Persists Among Tea Partiers, All Americans," April 14, 2010, accessed June 6, 2011, www.cbsnews.com/8301-503544_162-20002539-503544.html.

7. Dalia Sussman and Marina Stefan, "Obama and the 'Birthers' in the Latest Poll," The Caucus: The Politics and Government Blog of the New York Times, April 21, 2010, accessed June 6, 2011, thecaucus.blogs.nytimes.com/2010/04/21/obama-and-the-birthers-in-the-latest-poll, and "Born in the U.S.A.: The Truth About Obama's Birth Certificate," FactCheck.org, updated April 27, 2011, accessed June 6, 2011, www.factcheck.org/elections-2008/born_in_the_usa.html.

8. "Born Again Birther Party," The Progress Report, April 12, 2011, accessed June 6, 2011, pr.thinkprogress.org/2011/04/pr20110412.

9. "Donald, You're Fired! Trump Repeats False Claims About Obama's Birthplace," FactCheck.org, April 9, 2011, accessed June 6, 2011, factcheck.org/2011/04/ donald-youre-fired.

10. "Born Again Birther Party."

11. Alia Beard Rau, "Arizona Lawmakers OK Requiring Proof of Citizenship to Run for President," AZCentral.com, April 14, 2011, accessed June 6, 2011, www.azcentral.com/news/election/azelections/articles/2011/04/14/20110414arizona-lawmakers-approve-proof-of-citizenship-to-run-for-president.html#ixzz1Ji2j5r7x.

12. Dan Pfeiffer, "President Obama's Long Form Birth Certificate," The White House Blog, April 27, 2011, accessed June 6, 2011, www.whitehouse.gov/blog/2011/04/27/president-obamas-long-form-birth-certificate.

13. "Fewer Are Angry at Government, But Discontent Remains High: Republicans, Tea Party Supporters More Mellow," Pew Research Center for the People & the Press, March 3, 2011, accessed June 6, 2011, people-press.org/2011/03/03/fewer-are-angry-at-government-but-discontent-remains-high.

14. Ibid.

15. Office of the Press Secretary, "Remarks by the President in State of the Union Address," The White House, January 27, 2010, accessed June 6, 2011, www.whitehouse.gov/the-press-office/remarks-president-state-union-address.

16. Richard E. Cohen and Brian Friehl, "2009 Vote Ratings: Politics as Usual," *National Journal,* February 26, 2010, accessed June 6, 2011, www.nationaljournal.com/njmagazine/cs_20100227_3230.php. Article requires subscription to view.

17. Brendan Nyhan, "Why the 'Death Panel' Myth Wouldn't Die: Misinformation in the Health Care Reform Debate," *The Forum* 8, no. 3 (2010), accessed June 6, 2011, www.bepress.com/forum/vol8/iss1/art5.

18. Matthew C. Nisbet, "Communicating Climate Change: Why Frames Matter for Public Engagement," *Environment: Science and Policy for Sustainable Development,* March–April 2009, accessed July 17, 2011, www.environment

magazine.org/Archives/Back%20Issues/March-April%202009/Nisbet-full.html.

19. Ibid.

20. Ibid.

21. Ibid.

22. Ibid.

23. Ibid.

24. James H. Kuklinski, et al., "Misinformation and the Currency of Democratic Citizenship," *Journal of Politics*, 62:3 (August 2000), 792, accessed June 6, 2011, www.uvm.edu/~dguber/POLS234/articles/kuklinski.pdf.

25. Nyhan, 3.

26. Brooks Jackson and Kathleen Hall Jamieson, *unSpun: Finding Facts in a World of Disinformation* (New York: Random House, 2007), 76.

27. Brian J. Gaines, et al., "Same Facts, Different Interpretations: Partisan Motivation and Opinion on Iraq," *Journal of Politics*, 69:4, November 2007, 957.

28. Jackson and Jamieson, 76.

29. Kuklinski et al., 792.

30. Ibid.

31. Brendan Nyhan and Jason Reifler, *When Corrections Fail: The Persistence of Political Misperceptions* (prepublication version), 2010, accessed June 6, 2011, www-personal.umich.edu/~bnyhan/nyhan-reifler.pdf (see section Fall 2005: Study 1).

32. Cass Sunstein, *On Rumors: How Falsehoods Spread, Why We Believe Them, What Can Be Done* (New York: Farrar, Straus and Giroux, 2009), 47–48.

33. Nyhan and Reifler.

34. Sunstein, 48.

35. Alex Jones, *Losing the News: The Future of the News That Feeds Democracy* (New York: Oxford University Press, 2009), 1–27.

36. Ibid, 3.

37. Ibid, 4.

38. Ibid, 3–4.

39. Scott Rasmussen, "66% of Voters Are Angry at the Media," *Rasmussen Reports*, June 15, 2010, accessed June 6, 2011, www.rasmussenreports.com/public_content/politics/general_politics/june_2010/66_of_voters_are_angry_at_the_media.

40. Pew Project for Excellence in Journalism, "The State of the News Media: An Annual Report on American Journalism," 2009, Overview, accessed July 17, 2011, stateofthemedia.org/2009/overview/public-attitudes.

41. Jones, 27.

42. Personal Democracy Forum, New York 2010, Truth, Fact-checking and Online Media—panel discussion with Jay Rosen, Bill Adair, Julian Assange, Marc Ambinder, Brendan Greeley, accessed June 6, 2011, pdfnyc.civicolive.com/?s=Ambinder&submit=Go.

43. Jones, 83.

44. Marc Ambinder, "#PDF10: Truth Telling and Shaming," *The Atlantic*, June 3, 2010, accessed June 6, 2011, www.theatlantic.com/politics/archive/2010/06/pdf10-truth-telling-and-shaming/57608.

45. Jay Rosen, "My Simple Fix for the Messed Up Sunday Shows," Jay Rosen: My Public Notebook, December 27, 2009, accessed June 6, 2011, jayrosen.posterous.com/my-simple-fix-for-the-messed-up-sunday-shows.

46. Ibid.

47. Jodi Enda, "Capital Flight," *American Journalism Review*, June/July 2010, accessed June 6, 2011, www.ajr.org/Article.asp?id=4877.

48. Ibid.

49. Sunstein, 85.

50. Ibid, 6.

51. Ibid, 3, 6.

52. Ibid, 46.

53. Sargent, "Who Woulda Thunk It."

54. "About Us," FactCheck.org, accessed June 6, 2011, factcheck.org/about.

55. "About Us," techPresident.com, accessed July 17, 2011, techpresident.com/about/about-us.

CHAPTER 7

Charity Scams

Craig Thompson

On January 12, 2010, a 7.0 earthquake shook parts of Haiti and its capital, Port-Au-Prince. More than 200,000 people died, more than 2 million were displaced, and property damage ran in the hundreds of millions of dollars, wreaking devastation in a country already struggling with financial hardship.

Foreign aid from other countries, nonprofits, and for-profit entities arrived quickly even as rattling aftershocks continued. But just as quickly, criminals began to take advantage of the tragedy by creating nonexistent charities to siphon money to their dubious causes. Within days of the quake, Frederick Ray McCoy of Atlanta registered at least three Haiti-related websites: DonateToHaitiNow.org, SupportHaiti Now.org, and HaitiNeedsU.org, claiming the funds raised through these domains would go to a private foundation that had not yet received formal federal tax-exempt status to be recognized as a charity.[1] Unable to raise much cash from the sites and scam the public, McCoy, an ex-con, scammed his web designer instead. Given the ownership of the domain names in lieu of payment for his services, Atlanta-based Baruch Walker had been led to believe he could sell the URLs on eBay as compensation for his work; the three sites remain unsold, and no money has ever been raised through these sites to help Haitians in need.[2]

Around the same time, BBC News undertook an investigation into a group of scammers from the U.K. who flooded people's email inboxes soliciting donations for Haitian relief. The emails had official-looking logos, with one going so far as to claim it came from the British Red Cross. They used phone numbers and street addresses for their charities within the email body that were later determined to be fakes.[3] Eight

133

days after the earthquake, the Charity Commission, which registers and regulates charities in the U.K., sent out a press release urging people to be vigilant about ensuring the validity of charitable appeals. Elsewhere around the globe, scammers sought donations by using the phone or trying to extract money face-to-face.

The Role of Government Agencies

In the U.S., the Federal Bureau of Investigation (FBI), with extensive knowledge of charity fraud following both the World Trade Center attacks on September 11, 2001, and Hurricane Katrina in September 2005, issued a press release the day after the earthquake hit Haiti. The release stated:

> The FBI today reminds internet users who receive appeals to donate money in the aftermath of Tuesday's earthquake in Haiti to apply a critical eye and do their due diligence before responding to those requests. Past tragedies and natural disasters have prompted individuals with criminal intent to solicit contributions purportedly for a charitable organization and/or a good cause.
>
> Therefore, before making a donation of any kind, consumers should adhere to certain guidelines, to include the following:
>
> * Do not respond to any unsolicited (spam) incoming emails, including clicking links contained within those messages.
>
> * Be skeptical of individuals representing themselves as surviving victims or officials asking for donations via email or social networking sites.
>
> * Verify the legitimacy of nonprofit organizations by utilizing various internet-based resources that may assist in confirming the group's existence and its nonprofit status rather than following a purported link to the site.
>
> * Be cautious of emails that claim to show pictures of the disaster areas in attached files because the files may

contain viruses. Only open attachments from known senders.

- Make contributions directly to known organizations rather than relying on others to make the donation on your behalf to ensure contributions are received and used for intended purposes.

- Do not give your personal or financial information to anyone who solicits contributions: Providing such information may compromise your identity and make you vulnerable to identity theft.

Anyone who has received an e-mail referencing the above information or anyone who may have been a victim of this or a similar incident should notify the IC3 [Internet Crime Complaint Center] via www.ic3.gov.[4]

In August 2010, a major flood damaged vast areas of Pakistan, displacing up to 20 million people. Checking Google in early September 2010 using the terms *flood*, *Pakistan*, and *charity*, people could find legitimate organizations advertising for relief funds among the new listings for organizations that offered to distribute assistance to victims. Almost immediately, the Charity Commission in the U.K. issued warnings about possible scams, and the website Charity Navigator listed 10 legitimate organizations already on the ground there as well as instructions on how to tell if a charity is bona fide.[5] Forbes.com suggested another way to determine the effectiveness of a charity set up after a natural disaster:

There are questions to be asked even if the site or the organization behind it asking for money is not run by scamsters. For instance, can the people behind a brand new U.S. website, www.HelpPakistan.com, which lists a Culver City, Calif. address and was registered on August 15, do better work on the ground in Pakistan than one of the large established international aid groups like the Red Cross? Yousuf Keekeebhai, a 37-year-old U.S. citizen of Pakistani origin who helped create the site, said the purpose was more to inform rather than raise money, although links are offered for would-be donors.[6]

The IC3, through a partnership among the FBI, National White Collar Crime Center, and the Bureau of Justice Assistance, established a 1-866 hotline that was staffed 24/7 to handle calls about suspected fraud associated with relief efforts. Shortly thereafter, in March 2010, when a major earthquake hit Chile, the hotline was expanded.

There is a pattern here: Large-scale disasters tend to bring out charity scammers. This was certainly true after Hurricane Katrina destroyed parts of New Orleans in 2005. The Center for Public Integrity keeps a list of fraud cases involving damage from the hurricane.[7] One case involves Gary Kraser, who set up a fraudulent charity, AirKatrina.com, to solicit funds for air fuel. According to a grand jury indictment filed in the U.S. Southern District of Florida, "Air Katrina was a 'group of Florida pilots' who were 'flying medical supplies into Louisiana,' 'transporting children in need of immediate medical attention,' and 'donating their time, cargo space & resources to the victims of Hurricane Katrina.'"[8] The indictment charged that these were all fraudulent activities, and Kraser was charged with four counts of wire fraud after accepting funds across state lines. Kraser pled guilty to one count of wire fraud and was sentenced to 21 months in prison.

In February 2006, months after the hurricane, Florida's then-attorney general, Charlie Crist, filed a deceptive trade lawsuit against Robert Moneyhan, who had set up the following URLs (while using the alias Demon Moon at his local post office) after the disaster: KatrinaHelp.com, KatrinaDonations.com, KatrinaRelief.com, and KatrinaReliefFund.com. Within the civil action, case 05-CA-381, Crist noted that Moneyhan had not "applied for or obtained appropriate registration to permit solicitation of donations" and noted that "this is not a legitimate charity and any money raised would not go to the victims." Moneyhan lost the civil suit, was ordered to pay $10,000, and was not to use any Katrina-related websites in the future.

Fraud became so problematic following the hurricane that the Hurricane Katrina Fraud Task Force was created to track down the scammers. The task force's "First Year Report to the Attorney General" in September 2006 described this type of scam:

> The first cycle of fraud—charity-fraud schemes—begins at (or even shortly before) the time that a disaster strikes. With Katrina and Rita, for example, criminals exploited the outpouring of private and public support for hurricane victims by obtaining domain names for websites and then establishing fraudulent websites to which they tried to persuade the public to send their charitable donations for hurricane victims. The lifecycle for these charity-fraud schemes extends from the onset of the disasters for four to six weeks thereafter.[9]

These issues seem to be improving. After the March 2011 earthquake and tsunami in northeast Japan that brought homelessness and property losses to thousands of people and caused billions of dollars in damage, most of the online postings encouraging charitable contributions issued warnings about how to avoid charity scams and gave direct contacts for organizations that could provide on-the- ground assistance. These warnings came not only from media orga-nizations worldwide, but also from the U.S. government. The FBI issued a warning as early as March 14, 2011, just 3 days after the events.[10]

And, days after the devastating Mississippi River floods of May 2011, the Federal Trade Commission issued warnings to avoid both charity and home repair scams.[11]

Other Watchdogs

Internet users are constantly being bombarded with sympathy-seeking emails asking them to contribute to a wide swath of causes. A website called Hoax-Slayer keeps an ongoing log of email hoaxes, a list that never seems short of items.[12] In mid-2010, the site reported on spam mail about Baby Manuela, a child with an unspecified "very rare disease." Readers are asked to forward the email to three people, after which 32 cents per forwarded email are supposedly donated toward the child's operation. Another email claims that the Make-A-Wish Foundation will donate 7 cents toward the medical bills of a sick child named Amirtha each time the email is forwarded. Yet another email claims that AOL will donate 5 cents to Nirosha Silva, whose husband was apparently paralyzed in a horrific car accident, every time the email is forwarded. And another email claims that the Make-A-Wish Foundation will also donate 7 cents to Matt Dawson, a cancer victim, every time the message is forwarded. The Make-A-Wish Foundation posted a response on its website to these chain letters, stating that "each day, the Make-A-Wish Foundation and its chapters receive hundreds of inquiries about chain letters claiming to be associated with the Foundation and featuring sick children. However, we do not participate in these kinds of wishes."[13] The foundation then goes on to outline actions that internet users can take: "Inform the sender that the foundation does not participate in chain letter wishes; Refer the sender and all recipients to this page; Do not forward the chain letter; Refer senders to ways they can help the Foundation." In addition, another internet fraud watchdog site, Scambusters.org, offered these tools to handle email charity solicitations:

Unless you have signed up to receive email from a charity, do not respond to email charity solicitations. Real charities do not normally recruit new donors by email, and especially not by spaham (misspelled intentionally).

Email charity scams may use legitimate sounding names and link to a website where you can make a donation. These tend to be fake websites made to look like an organization's official site.

Be wary of websites that ask for personal information like your Social Security number, date of birth or bank account information, which can lead to identity theft.

Action: If you want to help the charity mentioned in the email, contact them directly with a phone call or use a Google search to find their real website.

More and more charities are accepting donations made on their official websites, so it's not wrong to make a donation this way. Just don't use an unsolicited email to get there.[14]

In the era of the internet, one of the main moneymakers for search engines is ad serving, which offers up a set of links that are connected to the search terms entered into the search bar. Ingenious for advertisers and search engines, yes, but when it comes to online charities, these links are a potential minefield.

A mid-2010 search for *Help Haiti* in the Google search engine is illustrative. On the right side of the screen is a set of Sponsored Links to sites including UNICEF USA and World Vision, both reputable charities. But there were also links to FindYourMission.org ("rebuild Haiti schools"), ArtNet.com ("Charity sale on ArtNet"), and PeachFurFleece.com ("Fleece Blankets for Haiti"). In the results for the same search in Bing, Microsoft's search engine, links to UNICEF USA and Oxfam America reside next to a link to Food for the Poor ("Help in Haiti") and even a link to eBay ("Buy Help Haiti. You may get 8% off with PayPal if eligible."). The takeaway from these examples is that just because sites come up as Sponsored Links as part of a web search does not necessarily mean they are legitimate. If you are interested in donating through any of the sites that appear as AdSense links, be sure to use due diligence via the techniques described in the section "Resources for Defeating Fraud."

Whether inspired by natural disasters or deadly illnesses (real or imaginary), all of these attempts to extract money from unsuspecting donors share one thing: It is alarmingly simple to conduct a little bit of research into any website or group to determine its legitimacy. Scammers hope that people will not take this additional step.

Detecting and Defeating Fraud

On the surface, detecting internet charity scams can seem difficult. The scammers are sharing online space with legitimate organizations that are using the web as a simpler, more effective way of raising money for their causes. And again, the scammers are relying on people's trustworthy natures to meet their end goal: fraudulently collecting money in the name of a good cause.

However, there are a number of red flags that, if raised, should create some doubt in the mind of the potential internet donor:

- Email solicitations that appear in your spam box

- Suspicious URLs

- Requests for personal information

In appealing to the empathetic side of human nature, charity scammers are relying on a single assumption: "There's no way this person could be scamming me, especially in this time of great crisis." This assumption has been proven time and again to be incorrect.

While empathy is a powerful force, common sense and a small amount of due diligence can ensure that your donation heads to a reliable and valid source. Take the following steps to scam-proof your donation.

Being skeptical of email is particularly important. Legitimate organizations do solicit funds via email so it's important to be vigilant about the originating email address. Many times, a scammer will mention a legitimate charity in the body of an email, sometimes going so far as to embed the charity's logo within the email body. Ensure that the email is sent from a legitimate email address. For example, an email from the Red Cross should come from an email address ending in *redcross.org* or some local variant thereof such as *nyred cross.org*. If an email is soliciting you for something for the Red Cross, be careful if it *does not* originate from a legitimate email address.

Links from scammers generally either lead the internet user to a bogus website or contain a virus that could harm your computer or even steal pieces of your identity. A key element in determining if you should donate to a charity—whether you found it via email, a website, or a sponsored Google link—is to do a bit of research on the charity. This should clear up any doubts you might have about donating.

Resources for Defeating Fraud

A key charity research site is Charity Navigator (www.charitynavigator. org), which bills itself as "Your Guide to Intelligent Giving." A nonprofit funded by individuals, corporations, and foundations, Charity Navigator was founded in 2001 to keep tabs on the nonprofit sector by analyzing financial documents provided by charities. To date, it has evaluated more than 5,000 charities.

Charity Navigator's homepage has a search bar. If you enter the name of an organization into the charity search bar, the site provides ratings based on organizational efficiency, organizational capacity, and the like. According to Charity Navigator, Food For The Poor, a charity mentioned earlier as one of the Bing ad-serving sites, earned the group's highest rating—four stars out of four—based on its low percentage of donations going to administrative costs and its organizational capacity. Charity Navigator also notes whether the charity has a Donor Privacy Policy, a financial statement, and a mission statement, and it provides a link to the charity's official site and contact information.[15]

Another place to investigate a charity is the Better Business Bureau (BBB; www.bbb.org/us). On its website, the BBB has posted the document "The BBB Wise Giving Alliance Standards for Charity Accountability," which outlines in fine detail the steps a charity needs to take to earn approval from the BBB.[16] This document outlines all of the compliance factors a charity needs to follow in order to meet the BBB's quality standards, including information on financial statements, administrative costs, member salaries, governance, etc. The materials were recently updated with references to online solicitations and the charity's use of a website. In essence, a charity's website, if it is seeking online solicitations, has to contain the same information that is submitted to the BBB to meet compliance:

> Include on any charity websites that solicit contributions, the same information that is recommended for annual reports, as well as the mailing address of the charity and electronic access to its most recent IRS Form 990.[17]

Whether or not a website is seeking solicitations, it still must contain the charity's privacy policy and a link to contact information.

A charity's posting on the BBB site will list the category Evaluation Conclusions midway on the search results page. This section will tell you whether the charity has passed BBB muster based on its 20 charitable accountability standards. For example, Food for the Poor meets these standards. But Salesian Missions, the umbrella organization that runs Find Your Mission, does not have an evaluation on its page. Because of this, Salesian must be treated with skepticism; the BBB has written the following explanation in its notes about Salesian Missions:

> Despite written BBB Wise Giving Alliance requests in the past year, this organization either has not responded to

Alliance requests for information or has declined to be evaluated in relation to the Alliance's Standards for Charity Accountability. While participation in the Alliance's charity review efforts is voluntary, the Alliance believes that failure to participate may demonstrate a lack of commitment to transparency.[18]

In short, if you happen to look at a site such as KatrinaHelp.com and it does *not* show basic information such as the Internal Revenue Service (IRS) Form 990, then the site should be treated with suspicion, according to the BBB standards.[19]

A third place to look is CharityChoices.com. This is another watchdog site where users search through an alphabetical list of charities that this site deems "accountable." The site measures accountability using the 10 accountability standards from the federal government's Combined Federal Campaign (CFC).[20] These standards require a charity to do the following:

1. Reveal the percentage spent on fundraising and administrative costs.

2. Undergo an annual audit.

3. Prepare an annual report to the IRS.

4. Document the "health and human benefits" it has provided during the previous year.

5. Be recognized by the IRS as a 501(c)(3) public charity.

6. Have an "active and responsible governing body."

7. Be "truthful and non-deceptive" in how it promotes itself, making "no exaggerated or misleading claims."

8. Use donations "for the announced purposes of the charitable organization."

9. Prohibit the sale or lease of the names of its CFC contributors.

10. Demonstrate "a substantial local presence" to qualify as a local charity in one of the CFC's more than 300 campaigns across the country.

CharityChoices.com also allows charities to answer six questions it provides, further validating the charities' existence:

1. Why do you exist?

2. What have you accomplished?

3. How do you help people in my community?

4. Why do you need my support?

5. How can I be sure you will use my money wisely and won't waste it?

6. Can I volunteer? How?

Answers to these questions should provide valuable insights into the validity of a charity.

Yet another resource to investigate a suspected site or charity is the American Institute of Philanthropy's Charity Watch (www.charity watch.org), which keeps an eye on 500 charities and publishes the "Charity Rating Guide & Watchdog Report."[21] For $40, you can buy a detailed analysis, including contact information and financial performance measurements for these charities, as well as an overall grade.

Those seeking information can also turn to GuideStar (www.guidestar.org), which is a database of more than 1.8 million nonprofits aiming to provide transparency to the nonprofit sector. To this end, the site publishes a robust amount of content on a particular charity, including contact information, mission and impact statements, financial statements, and Form 990s provided either by the charity itself or by the IRS.

IRS Form 990

IRS Form 990 is the government form that most nonprofits must complete and submit in order to obtain tax-exempt status. According to the Investigative Reporters and Editors organization, Form 990 is the "Rosetta Stone" for investigating nonprofits. GuideStar publishes the 990s for more than 5 million charities, and while a regular user will most likely not have the time to comb through an entire 990 (which can run up to 37 pages), the mere presence of a 990 from a nonprofit is a good thing. However, some organizations are exempt from having to provide 990s: faith-based organizations, groups with less than $25,000 in annual income, and subsidiary organizations of larger organizations.

Form 990 was reorganized in 2009. Now, following an overview and summary of financials, a charity can describe its outreach efforts (page 2). The new form requires charities to reveal executive compensation on page 7, rather than on a separate Schedule A as in the past, and it also requires them to report when a former or current employee has been paid $100,000 or more. For the regular user looking into a charity, this will provide further insight as to whether it is legitimate.

A Brief Guide to Protecting Yourself From Online Scams

Charity Navigator has created a very useful five-point summary of how to avoid online scams, provided here.[22]

Do not respond to email solicitations. Unless you've signed up to receive a charity's electronic communications, be skeptical of email solicitations. Although you may receive an email that appears to come from a valid organization, as a general rule legitimate organizations do not solicit funds through email. Despite how official an email may seem it could very well be a scam. Many scams use the names of actual organizations and include a link to a website where you can make a donation. Do not follow any links within the message; these tend to be fake websites that are made to look like the organization's official site. Email solicitations may also include information about a foreign bank account where you can send your contribution. An organization requesting that you send funds to a foreign bank is always bogus.

If you are interested in donating to the charity mentioned in the email, initiate contact directly with the organization. Type out the organization's web address or call them directly. This will ensure that you have reached the organization for which you intend to make a donation.

Delete unsolicited emails with attachments. Never respond to unsolicited emails, commonly referred to as spam. Do not open any attachments to these emails even if they claim to contain pictures of a particular tragedy. These attachments are probably viruses.

Be leery of people that contact you online claiming to be a victim. Anyone alleging to be in this position is most likely part of a scam. People affected by a disaster or afflicted by a disease are in no position to contact you directly for assistance.

Seek out the charity's authorized website. The results of a general web search on Google, Yahoo!, or another search engine may include a fraudulent site designed to look like a legitimate charity's website. For example, even before Hurricane Katrina made landfall, criminals were setting up websites that included the keyword Katrina (such as www.katrinahelp.com and www.katrinarelief.com) in an effort to collect money and personal information. In the weeks following the devastating storm, the FBI reported that it had identified over 4,000 bogus websites that were attempting to capitalize on the goodwill of generous Americans.

So, how can you determine if a site is valid? Start by examining the web address. Most nonprofit web addresses end with .org and not .com. Avoid web addresses that end in a series of numbers. Also, bogus sites often ask for detailed personal information such as your social security, date of birth, or your bank account and pin information. Be extremely skeptical of these sites as providing this information makes it easy for them to steal your identity.

Your best option is to start your web search at Charity Navigator. Our analysts have done the research for you. On each charity's ratings page we include a direct link to the organization's authorized website.

Give through a reputable and secure service. Charity Navigator recently added the convenience of online donating. For a trial period, donors no longer have to make the added effort of visiting a charity's authorized website to make an online gift. A simple click of a mouse, powered by Network for Good's secure giving system, enables donors to not only research, but also support the charities found on our site.

Don't be afraid to make a donation. Each year millions of dollars in online contributions make it safely to charitable organizations. As always, make sure that you're giving to an established, reputable organization.

How to Report a Possible Charity Scam

What should you do if you do suspect fraud and want to take the additional step of reporting the suspected site to the authorities? There are a few actions you can take at the state, federal, and self-help level. These steps are the same as if you were investigating an entity in the brick-and-mortar world:

- Once you have gathered all the information you can (who, what, where, when, and how), start by filing a complaint with the attorney general for your state.[23] Provide the information in writing along with the relevant documents and contact information for yourself.[24]

- You can also file a complaint with the secretary of state in your state.[25]

- You can also file complaints locally with the city or county prosecutor or the district attorney.

- You can also file complaints with the Federal Trade Commission[26] and the IRS.[27]

Keep an eye on dealings within the charity itself. For example, if on Form 990 you see funds being transferred between members of the charity's board of directors and trustees or if you notice loans made to a director or an officer of the charity, this activity is potentially fraudulent. In these cases, you can report your concerns to the attorney general of your state, to the IRS, and/or to the local district attorney in the district in which the charity resides. The IRS has the power to impose sanctions on individuals who abuse their positions of control over charities for personal benefit.

The BBB offers a link to file a complaint right on the homepage of its website. The BBB also offers a complaint form through its Wise Giving Alliance. The number of public inquiries received "helps identify which national charities will be the subject of a BBB Wise Giving Alliance report."[28]

One final place to check whenever you are suspicious of a scam or intentional misinformation is Urban Legends, also known as Snopes,[29] where rumors are debunked or confirmed (www.snopes.com).

In summary, there are a number of places to find information about suspected scams and ways to report them to the proper authorities. As the sergeant on *Hill Street Blues* used to say when concluding his morning briefing: "Be careful out there."

Endnotes

1. William P. Barrett, "Ex-Convict Registers Haiti Charity Web Addresses," Forbes.com, January 15, 2010, accessed June 7, 2011, www.forbes.com/2010/01/15/convict-haiti-relief-web-sites-personal-finance-charity-scams.html.

2. Telephone interview with Baruch Walker, April 19, 2010.

3. Razia Iqbal, "E-mail Scams Exploiting Haiti Earthquake Generosity," BBC News, February 16, 2010, accessed June 7, 2011, news.bbc.co.uk/2/hi/uk_news/8517243.stm.

4. U.S. Federal Bureau of Investigation, "Haitian Earthquake Relief Fraud Alert," January 13, 2010, accessed July 17, 2011, www.ic3.gov/media/2010/1001 13.aspx.

5. "Pakistan Floods," Charity Navigator, accessed June 7, 2011, www.charity navigator.org/index.cfm?bay=content.view&cpid=1132.

6. William P. Barrett, "Be Wary of Web Scams About Flood in Pakistan," Forbes.com, September 7, 2010, accessed June 7, 2011, blogs.forbes.com/williampbarrett/2010/09/07/be-wary-of-web-scams-about-flood-in-pakistan.

7. "Katrina Watch: Fraud," The Center for Public Integrity, accessed June 7, 2011, projects.publicintegrity.org/katrina/filter.aspx?cat=14.

8. *United States of America v. Kraser*, Case 1:05 cr 20745 filed in United States District Court, Southern District of Florida in Miami on September 29, 2005.

9. U.S. Department of Justice, "Hurricane Katrina Fraud Task Force: First Year Report to the Attorney General," September 2006, accessed June 7, 2011, www.justice.gov/criminal/katrina/docs/09-12-06AGprogressrpt.pdf.

10. FBI National Press Office, "Tips on Avoiding Fraudulent Charitable Contribution Schemes," Federal Bureau of Investigation, March 14, 2011, accessed June 7, 2011, www.fbi.gov/news/pressrel/press-releases/tips-on-avoiding-fraudulent-charitable-contribution-schemes.

11. "FTC Warns Consumers: Charity and Home Repair Scams May Appear After a Disaster," Federal Trade Commission, May 27, 2011, accessed June 7, 2011, www.ftc.gov/opa/2011/05/homerepair.shtm.

12. "Charity Hoaxes," Hoax-Slayer, accessed June 7, 2011, www.hoax-slayer.com/charity-hoaxes.html.

13. "Fraud Alerts," Make-A-Wish Foundation of America, accessed June 7, 2011, www.wish.org/about/fraud_alerts.

14. "Four Charity Scams to Avoid," Scambusters.org, accessed June 7, 2011, www.scambusters.org/charityscams.html.

15. "Food For The Poor," Charity Navigator, accessed June 7, 2011, www.charity navigator.org/index.cfm?bay=search.summary&orgid=3714.

16. "Standards for Charity Accountability," Better Business Bureau, 2003, accessed June 7, 2011, www.bbb.org/us/Charity-Standards.

17. "Better Business Bureau Report for Preble Street Resource Center," Better Business Bureau, September 2007–September 2009, accessed June 7, 2011, www.bbb.org/charity-reviews/boston/preble-street-resource-center-in-portland-me-6312.

18. "BBB Wise Giving Report for Salesian Missions," Better Business Bureau, October 2010–October 2011, accessed June 7, 2011, www.bbb.org/charity-reviews/national/religious/salesian-missions-in-new-rochelle-ny-161.

19. "Implementation Guide to BBB Wise Giving Alliance Standards for Charity Accountability," Better Business Bureau, accessed June 7, 2011, www.bbb.org/us/Charity-Evaluation. The Better Business Bureau is also located at www.give.org.

20. "10 Accountability Standards," CharityChoices.com, accessed June 7, 2011, www.charitychoices.com/cfc_stand.asp.

21. "Welcome," American Institute of Philanthropy, accessed June 7, 2011, www.charitywatch.org.

22. "Protecting Yourself From Online Scams," Charity Navigator, accessed June 7, 2011, www.charitynavigator.org/index.cfm?bay=content.view&cpid=313.

23. "The Attorneys General: Current Attorneys General," National Association of Attorneys General, accessed June 7, 2011, www.naag.org/current-attorneys-general.php.

24. For more about the process of filing complaints to the Attorney General check www.atg.wa.gov/fileacomplaint.aspx, accessed June 7, 2011.

25. National Association of Secretaries of State Contact Roster, accessed July 27, 2011, www.nass.org/index.php?option=com_contact_display&Itemid=346.

26. Federal Trade Commission, February 25, 2010, accessed June 7, 2011, www.ftc complaintassistant.gov.

27. "Criminal Enforcement," IRS.gov, March 14, 2011, accessed June 7, 2011, www.irs.gov/compliance/enforcement/index.html.

28. "About BBB Wise Giving Alliance," Better Business Bureau, accessed August 31, 2011, www.bbb.org/us/about-bbb-wga.

29. Snopes.com, accessed June 7, 2011, www.snopes.com.

Concluding Thoughts

Anne P. Mintz

One intent of this book is to enhance the reader's awareness of the subtleties and unintended consequences of living our lives online. The categories of intentionally misleading or manipulative misinformation covered in *Web of Deceit* occasionally manifest themselves in our lives in ways we haven't discussed. Some are so subtle that we don't notice them until they are pointed out to us.

For example, content in the textbooks used in public schools all across the United States can be deceptively incorrect. Between December 2010 and March 2011, the *Washington Post* published a series of articles documenting the discovery of blatantly erroneous information published in history textbooks used by schools in Virginia.[1] One of those errors was the purported "fact" that black slaves from Virginia had fought on the side of the Confederacy in the Civil War. The reviewer checking the quality of the manuscript had confirmed this to be true, having found it on the internet. This and other glaring errors were simply published as fact. In this case, the publisher agreed to correct the errors and replace the textbooks. But it's an area we don't usually think of when considering the dangers of intentional misinformation on the internet.

And some intentional misinformation doesn't fit into neat categories because it involves one or more of them.

A growing problem for law enforcement is the creation of sophisticated computer codes that allow the creators to engage in criminal activity on the internet across national borders. Fortunately, U.S. law enforcement officials have increasingly been able to bring criminal charges in this country that have resulted in convictions.

For example, in May 2010, the U.S. Federal Trade Commission shut down the internet firm 3FN, based in Belize, for aiding gangs that ran botnets, carried out phishing attacks, and traded in images of child pornography:

> At the Federal Trade Commission's request, a district court judge has permanently shut down a rogue internet Service Provider that recruited, hosted, and actively participated in the distribution of spam, spyware, child pornography, and other malicious and illegal content. The ISP's computer servers and other assets have been seized and will be sold by a court-appointed receiver, and the operation has been ordered to turn over $1.08 million in ill-gotten gains to the FTC. ... In filings with the district court, the FTC alleged that more than 4,500 malicious software programs were controlled by command-and-control servers hosted by 3FN. This malware included programs capable of key-stroke logging, password stealing, and data theft, programs with hidden backdoor remote control activity, and pro-grams involved in spam distribution.[2]

Internet users in all countries have fallen victim to this type of criminal activity; as we've shown in the preceding chapters, we are in need of active legal and technological protections.

The technology available to ordinary citizens enables the manipu-lation of truth, which is then spread as fact. There is often no inde-pendent corroboration of the facts in the rush to get the information out there. Information flows so quickly and in such huge quantities that all kinds of internet users—individuals, corporate executives, government officials, media editors, and television producers—have difficulty keeping up effectively. Nik Gowing of the Reuters Institute for the Study of Journalism at Oxford University puts it this way:

> As a result, there is a new vulnerability, fragility and brit-tleness of power which weakens both the credibility and accountability of governments, the security organs and corporate institutions. This is often at the precise moment, during a time of adversity, that public opinion expects the optimum official assessments and leadership.[3]

Far too often, we don't stop to think about the veracity of information before acting on it. We don't ask questions. We are on deadline. We need to get to the next item on our to-do list. The results can be disastrous: "No matter that the information ... being spread may be inaccurate, or only partly true ... leaders have to respond, and faster than used to be necessary," according to Gowing. "The new core challenge is the tyranny of the time line."[4]

Knowing how to think for ourselves and evaluate information is critical in a democracy, where citizens must be able to make the decisions that affect their lives. There are valid differences of opinion as to how we should govern ourselves, use technology, conduct business, educate our children, and help those in need. But first, we must find a way to agree on the facts upon which we base those decisions and opinions. And it is not just text that must be confirmed. Images, too, are no longer automatically believable because of the ubiquitous technologies available to alter them.

The complexity of all this activity has grown exponentially since the publication of *Web of Deception* in 2002 and was the catalyst for this new work. It is not the final word on the subject, unfortunately. Educators all over the world are teaching their students to think for themselves and to use good judgment when evaluating websites. Parents are becoming more diligent about supervising their children's online activities and are more informed about cyberbullying and other dangers that can lure their children into harm's way. Lawmakers are paying attention to the issues and trying to keep up with the technology. But the task seems never ending. What remains is that anyone using the internet is advised to exercise personal responsibility and sound thinking when online.

While the issues surrounding internet misinformation and manipulation are intensely complex, they are also remarkably simple. Forewarned is forearmed. Take your time. Check your facts. Proceed with caution.

Endnotes

1. A good summary of these articles is the one by Kevin Sieff, "Virginia Board of Education Withdraws Approval of Two History Textbooks," *Washington Post*, January 13, 2011, accessed June 7, 2011, www.washingtonpost.com/wp-dyn/content/article/2011/01/13/AR2011011307050.html.

2. "FTC Permanently Shuts Down Notorious Rogue Internet Service Provider," Federal Trade Commission, May 19, 2010, accessed June 7, 2011, www.ftc.gov/opa/2010/05/perm.shtm.

3. Nik Gowing, *Skyful of Lies and Black Swans: The New Tyranny of Shifting Information Power in Crises* (Oxford: Reuters Institute for the Study of Journalism, 2009), 6.

4. Ibid.

Evaluating Websites

Amber Benham

While surfing the internet, we are bombarded with a seemingly endless stream of information. Facts, figures, graphs, and spreadsheets—the sheer quantity of data at your fingertips is simultaneously empowering and frightening. But if you know what to look for in a reliable website, the internet will open doors you never knew existed. While there are no hard-and-fast rules, following these guidelines and using a critical eye to evaluate what you find—just like researching in a print library—will let your brain and your gut take you to the good stuff.

What to Check For
The Author

Using the internet as a research tool requires no less diligence than a journalist would use while conducting a live interview. Asking questions is just the first step. Once a subject provides you with answers, you must take a critical look at the source to determine how trustworthy this newfound information is. If you don't trust the source, you can't trust the answers.

When you visit a webpage, first consider who wrote what you are reading. If it's an article, the author's name is likely to be listed under the headline, just as in traditional print stories; if you're lucky, the author's name will also feature a hyperlink that will connect you to an author bio page. There you might find the author's educational background, links to other stories he or she has written, and various ways to contact him or her. This is the best-case scenario. Here all you have to do is follow up on what you find to determine whether to trust the source.

In many cases, you may run across documents authored by an anonymous writer, someone using a nickname, or who self-identifies by first name only. This is trickier. If it's a blog, try visiting the About Me/Us section. If you cannot identify the author, it would not be wise to put much confidence in the posted content.

Once you've identified the author, it's time to take another look at that bio and consider those qualifications. First, is this person an expert in the subject that is being discussed? Don't fall for the general expert trap. Being famous or an expert in something doesn't necessarily qualify a person to write about a different subject. Does the author have any training or formal education in this subject that adds credibility to the content? Does this person have any obvious conflicts of interest in writing about this subject?

Often celebrity status is confused with expertise. For example, an actress with an eating disorder may be an expert if we're talking about performing on stage or screen, but she is not necessarily an expert if the subject being discussed is how to achieve and maintain a healthy weight.

An individual may have access to important facts but still may not meet the criteria for being a reliable source. A politician who failed to capture enough votes in the last election might have valuable knowledge about the inner workings of campaign fundraising. However, this doesn't mean that the candidate can be trusted to analyze the flaws objectively in our current campaign finance regulations. There may be a conflict of interest at work. Looser regulations could mean more financial support for an upcoming campaign, which could improve the chances of winning. Imagine this candidate says that campaign finance restrictions violate our right to free speech. Perhaps that is true, but this opinion would carry more weight if it came from a constitutional law professor than perhaps from a career politician who might stand to benefit from loosened regulations.

Some websites use only freelance writers. For example, About.com publishes articles on just about every topic imaginable. Since the site has a limited editorial staff, you must evaluate the individual writers on their own merits. With About.com in particular, each article has a link to the author's bio page where you can find information about the author's educational background, work experience, and awards or recognitions he or she has received. With freelancers, it's important to consider the author's expertise in the specific subject matter. You should also ask what else this author has written and for whom.

Be cautious of sites that rely on crowdsourcing, or reader contributions, to maintain their pages. For example, Wikipedia allows literally anyone, with some exceptions, to change, update, add to, or delete content on its pages. This doesn't mean the site or a given page is without merit. However, rather than taking content on the site at face value, be sure to follow the source notes at the bottom of the page and confirm the information yourself.

The Publisher

When evaluating whether a website offers reliable information, consider the reputation of the publisher. Often who the publisher is can reveal as much, if not more, about the validity of information on the page.

For instance, if the National Institutes of Health (NIH) publishes a document about diabetes, we can assume that the information in this document is objective and medically sound, even if no specific author is credited. Since NIH is a well-respected research institution with a solid medical reputation, we can trust documents about diabetes that it chooses to publish. In this case, the publisher's reputation helps support the validity of a document.

In other instances, the publisher can be the very reason to doubt a document. For example, imagine that a highly regarded online magazine specializing in "the good life" publishes a story about how smoking cigars has been shown to decrease the risk of diabetes. Based on the publisher's reputation as a magazine known for its sexy cover models and stories about sex, alcohol, and adult leisure activities, a skeptical researcher might question the information in this article. Of course, it's possible that a staff writer at this publication researched diabetes with several medical professionals and that all the facts in the article are accurate, but the publisher's reputation alone is not enough to quell any skepticism. We must consider other factors before we can trust this article.

Sometimes a publisher can be known and respected, yet not be a dependable source for objective information. For instance, each U.S. senator publishes a website, which no doubt offers accurate contact information for the senator, the correct dates for elections, and useful information on how to register to vote. But imagine if a senator's homepage features a story on the hot-button issue of immigration with the following quote: "Bill XI98a will reduce the flow of undocumented children that currently overwhelm our public schools and cost taxpayers $30 million each year." Let's consider the senator's purpose for publishing this statement. Surely one goal is to keep constituents abreast of government activities, but senators are not indifferent participants in our government. They also have political agendas and opinions that inform their work. Another purpose for an elected official to publish content to an official website is to garner support for his or her political goals. This doesn't mean the site can't be trusted, but it does mean you need to consider the purpose of any information that has been included. A link to a voter registration form needn't raise any suspicions, but a claim that taxpayers are spending $30 million on undocumented children—a controversial issue—should be investigated further. The senator may have included this statistic to persuade readers to support his or her bill. Where did the figure come from? Does the page provide a source to verify the number?

At other times, a publisher's motive may not be so obvious. Be sure to read any sections labeled Our Mission, Our Purpose, or Our Philosophy. While it isn't necessary that the publisher be objective on all issues, it should be clear what point of view the publisher has, if any. Keeping that perspective in mind helps a critical researcher determine what information can be trusted and what needs to be verified using another source.

Contrary to popular belief, there is no application process for people who wish to host a website. Of all the domain extensions, only three are restricted to particular groups: .gov (government agencies), .edu (educational institutions), and .mil (military departments). But don't assume just because a URL ends in .org that the website is operated by a nonprofit organization. Anyone can start a .com, .org, or .net. A case in point is the www.martinlutherking.org site that is sponsored by the White Supremacist group Stormfront; this is *not* a registered nonprofit organization (see the Introduction and Chapter 3 for more information).

Sometimes it can be difficult if not impossible to figure out who the publisher is by visiting the site. First, try looking for a link or tab on the homepage labeled About, Contact Us, or Who We Are. If you cannot find contact or ownership information within the site, visit Alexa.com, NetworkSolutions.com, or any site that links to a "whois" database to find out who owns the domain. There you will find the name and contact information for the domain owner, as well as data about the site's launch date, how much traffic it gets, and how many people link to the site. If your search finds the domain but no ownership information and the site doesn't provide any contact information, this website should not be trusted. Relying on information from this site would be much the same as believing what you overhear from strangers on your morning commute.

The Content

After examining the author and publisher, take a closer look at the actual content of the website.

First, consider the quality of the writing. How the content is written speaks volumes about the trustworthiness of the information. Bad writing (i.e., writing with grammatical mistakes, errors in word usage, or incorrect punctuation) tends to correspond to bad content. This seeming lack of professionalism is a red flag. Though bad writing can be a flag for unreliable content, do not assume that the converse is true: Not all good writing can be trusted.

Second, note how the material is presented. Is it objective, or is there an obvious slant to what is being said? If there is a slant or bias, how might it affect the material? For instance, you come across an article in which a sports medicine doctor in southern California raves about the benefits of wearing insoles while running and promises faster marathon finish times if you wear one of his patented shoe inserts. You notice an obvious bias in favor of wearing shoe inserts and a lack of data to support the claims that such devices actually improve running performance. In this case, the bias is reason enough to be suspicious of the material. It would be unwise to rely on a doctor who touts a product that he sells and who stands to profit from his advice.

Be sure to look for any obvious holes in coverage by comparing a document to what you know and what you've read in other sources on the same topic. Suppose you are reading an article about how to keep white clothes white. It mentions stain treatment and detergent, but nothing about separating bold colors from whites, which was a major focus in all the other articles you've read; you will probably want to look for a better source.

Another factor to consider is the currency of the content. There are no set rules about how often a site needs to be updated, but a little common sense goes a long way. Consider that you are looking at a website that offers information about how to get tested and treated for HIV/AIDS. The content seems to be objective, complete, and well-written, but when you look closely, you see the information was posted on January 15, 1996. Clearly, our knowledge of HIV/AIDS has improved since 1996, and testing and treatment procedures have surely changed. In this case, the information is too outdated to be useful.

Now let's say instead of HIV/AIDS, you are researching Dante's *Divine Comedy*. You stumble upon a site hosted by a popular state university and find what seems to be a great article written by a resident English professor about the exact theme you were hoping to write about. You check the professor's bio and find that she has a PhD in Italian literature and has published extensively on Dante's works. But this article was also published in 1996. Is the information in this article outdated? Probably not. Considering that Dante wrote his masterpieces more than 700 years ago, it's unlikely much has changed in the last two decades that would impact our understanding of the themes in his writing.

Aside from the words on the page, be sure to examine any supporting links, documents, or references that are mentioned. The quality and currency of these supporting materials will reveal a great deal about how much effort the author put into creating accurate, well-balanced content. If there are links to other sites or documents, follow them. Make sure they work and connect you to content that is as current and as high a quality as the material you are trying to evaluate. You don't want to find out later that the entire article you are reading was based on decades-old statistics or a single sentence in a gossip blog.

If there are graphs, charts, or other visual representations of data, be careful not to take them at face value. A good site will not only provide the visual aids, but it will also offer information about the methodology used to create them. Be sure to ask, "Where did this figure come from?"

Last, but certainly not least, make sure the content is accurate. If you spot a factual error on a webpage, you absolutely don't want to count on anything else you read there. Not all mistakes are intentional, but if someone does a bad job of fact-checking one detail, you can't be sure that the other details have been confirmed either. So if the site you are evaluating says Barack Obama was elected on November 2, 2004, start looking for a new source.

The Look of the Site

As discussed in the previous section on publishers, there is very little control over who can publish what kind of page on the internet. This leaves researchers struggling to sort personal pages from commercial, informational from advocacy, and news from entertainment. In many cases, the appearance of a site can be a great indicator of what kind of page it is.

When there is advertising on a site, it should be clearly distinguished from content. If not, you may be viewing a page that pays writers to write positive reviews of its products or push a personal agenda. Be sure to note what kinds of ads are featured on the page. The presence of advertising by a company that might have a vested interest in selling to people perusing the site doesn't mean the site is biased or in any way tainted for taking such advertising support. But if the ads you see don't line up with what you'd expect to see on this kind of site, take note. Since many ads on the internet link to porn sites or other inappropriate content, take note of these as well.

A site owned by an established organization will usually feature that group's logo or watermark somewhere on the page. (For example, the official website for the Human Rights Campaign features the familiar yellow equal sign inside a solid blue square.) If you don't see an organization's logo somewhere on the page, the site might not be owned or endorsed by whom it says it is.

Certain timely occasions such as presidential elections provoke a rash of faux official sites. Sometimes the owners of these pages hope to discredit the reputation of someone who is currently in the limelight, while others aim to garner support. If you are researching someone who has recently become more famous, it may be helpful to see what the site looked like a few months or even years ago. The Wayback Machine (www.archive.org), also called the Internet Archive, lets you see archived websites at various points in history.

Finally, look at every URL to ensure the domain name and the extension are appropriate for the content. If you want to view a government website, be sure the domain extension is .gov. If you want to view a business's website, make sure the company name is spelled correctly. Many times a scammer will link from a respectable-looking site to one that is not related to the original topic: Be on the lookout, because malware can easily be downloaded into your hard drive or your identity can be stolen. Always be aware of the URL of the site you are viewing.

Social Networking Sites as Reference Tools

In the last few years, social networking sites have found a new home in the researcher's toolbox. Sites such as LinkedIn, Twitter, and Facebook offer tremendous insight into the personal lives of all kinds of individuals—students, professionals, and even celebrities—and make it possible to connect with communities of people that only exist online. Need to find members of the 1999 graduating class at Kingsborough Community College (KBCC)? Forget the yearbook. Just sign into Facebook and search on the KBCC network.

Remember that this newfound wealth of formerly private information doesn't come without a cost. First of all, people have a variety of motivations for what they post about themselves online. They may lie to impress a future employer or a date. They might change the year they graduated from school to appear younger than they actually are. Since there are no fact checkers on social networking sites, information found there should be taken as leads, not answers. Once you uncover information that may be valuable for your research, follow up and confirm what you've read. Chapter 1 in this book covers intentional misinformation on social media; read it carefully.

Some Sample Sites to Practice Evaluating

Before you start your own research, visit the following sites and use the guidance in this chapter to decide how trustworthy each one is:

- usa.gov

- usa.com

- www.barackobama.org

- www.martinlutherking.org

- www.justiceforimmigrants.org

- abortionchangesyou.com/explore

- www.monsanto.com

- sustainableagriculture.net

- www.sare.org

Ask yourself: Who wrote this article? Who sponsors the site? Is there an agenda to the content? Is it complete, accurate, and current? What kind of page is it? Is the URL appropriate for the kind of content on the site?

The internet is a powerful tool with a tremendous amount of information to offer, but *verify, verify, verify* is still the name of the game. When you take all that you've investigated into consideration, count on your instincts to tell you whether you can trust the information you've found. Don't take shortcuts, and remember: Buyer beware—even if it isn't money that's changing hands.

The Technologies of Deceit:
An Annotated Glossary

Deborah A. Liptak

Acknowledgment

Unless otherwise noted, all definitions in this Appendix are from the following sources:

U.S. Department of Defense, "DOD Dictionary of Military and Associated Terms," www.dtic.mil/doctrine.

U.S. Government Accountability Office, "Critical Infrastructure Protection: Key Private and Public Cyber Expectations Need to Be Consistently Addressed, Table 2: Types of Cyber Exploits," July 2010, www.gao.gov/new.items/d10628.pdf.

U.S. Government Accountability Office, "Cybersecurity for Critical Infrastructure Protection, Table 6: Threats to Critical Infrastructure," May 2004, www.gao.gov/new.items/d04321.pdf.

U.S. National Communications System, "Cyber Vulnerabilities Within the National Infrastructure's Supervisory Control and Data Acquisition Systems," May 2005, www.ncs.gov/library/tech_bulletins/2005/tib_05-4.pdf.

How Are Attacks Carried Out?
Abuse of Privilege

The most dangerous type of attack comes from someone who has willfully been given access within a system and then proceeds to abuse those privileges for his or her own purposes.

Chris Pick, vice president of productions and marketing at NetIQ and a former auditor with Ernst & Young, stated that organizations need to monitor their privileged users. "Granting privileges increases people's power. Access to computer systems needs to be matched to the role. Some people may have too many privileges and too much access for the job they do. Can they do more than they should in their role?"[1]

Deception or Masquerade

According to a technical report from the National Communications System, "After an attacker successfully breaches the security of a system, there are several classes of activities that an intruder can utilize to accomplish their goal ... Playing upon the trust that is placed in proper network operation, attackers can reconfigure the switch as they see fit to serve their purposes."[2]

Ian Fette, part of the Google Security Team, warns computer users about phishing attacks using a masquerade tactic. "The concept behind such an attack is pretty simple: Someone masquerades as someone else in an effort to fool you into sharing personal or other sensitive information with them. Phishers can masquerade as just about anyone, including banks, email and application providers, online merchants, online payment services, and even governments."[3]

Denial of Service

"Quickly growing in occurrence, Denial of Service (DoS) occurs when a system does not provide the function for which it is intended. This can occur due to reconfiguration or, more commonly, due to a maliciously overloaded system."[4] One method of attack denies system access to legitimate users without actually having to compromise the targeted system. From a single source, the attack overwhelms the target computer with messages and blocks legitimate traffic. It can prevent one system from being able to exchange data with other systems or prevent the system from using the internet.

A Distributed Denial of Service (DDoS) is a variation of DoS. It uses a coordinated attack from a distributed system of computers rather than a single source. Worms are often spread to multiple computers, which then attack the target. Network hacking is a technique used to bring down a network by creating superfluous traffic, clogging and congesting the pathways for data. Mass confusion results from DDoS attacks.

DoS doesn't require any hacking into a computer. Rather, it overwhelms the site with visitors. In July 2010, U.S. government websites, the New York Stock Exchange website, and several South Korean websites experienced DoS attacks.

In 1999, a series of coordinated attacks on American computers was traced to a computer in Moscow. (However, it has not been officially determined if the attacks originated in Moscow.) In 2003, the U.S. government began experiencing attacks on American computer systems. These attacks are believed to have originated with Chinese military hackers. Many U.S. computer networks, including Lockheed Martin, Sandia National Laboratories, Redstone Arsenal, and NASA, were affected for several years.

Users of the social networking site Twitter had a rough day on Thursday, August 6, 2009, when DDoS attacks shut down the site for 2 hours. Facebook, LiveJournal, and Google allegedly experienced glitches that same day.[5]

Eavesdropping or Wiretapping

With sufficient access to a data network, an attacker can view or hear all of the communicated contents of private data, telephone conversations, and so forth via eavesdropping or wiretapping. Keyboard emanations can also be detected with keystroke-sensing equipment.

It has long been known that electronic eavesdroppers could detect emanations from typewriter keystrokes. But in 2004, Dmitri Asonov and Rakesh Agrawal, computer security researchers for IBM, discovered that the same principle applies to computer keyboards. "It is now possible to eavesdrop on a typist's keystrokes and, by exploiting minute variations in the sounds made by different keys, distinguish and decipher what is being typed."[6]

Electromagnetic Pulse

A form of energy that exhibits wave-like behavior as it travels through space, an electromagnetic pulse (EMP) is most commonly caused by a nuclear explosion that may combine with electrical or electronic systems to produce damaging current and voltage surges.

Information is one of the most important needs for individuals following any disruptive disaster. Whether the disaster is natural or manmade, individuals want to know what happened, and whether family members and friends are safe, and to be assured that the situation is under control. An EMP attack would cut off all electronic communication; this would most likely result in psychological trauma to many people. Reestablishing electronic communications is one of the most crucial tasks following an EMP attack.[7]

Espionage and Corporate Espionage

Espionage is the act of obtaining, delivering, transmitting, communicating, or receiving information about the national defense with an intent, or reason to believe, that the information may be used to the injury of the U.S. or to the advantage of any foreign nation. It is a violation of 18 United States Code 792-798 and Article 106, Uniform Code of Military Justice.

Wen Ho Lee, a scientist at Los Alamos Nuclear Laboratory, was the focus of a counterintelligence inquiry in 1998. The case of Wen Ho Lee brought national attention not only to security at the laboratories but also to the sharing of information among scientists.[8] Federal investigators were unable to prove these accusations, yet Lee pleaded guilty to one of 59 counts—improper handling of restricted data—as part of a plea settlement. In June 2006, Lee received $1.6 million from the federal government and five media organizations as part of a civil suit settlement.

Exploit Tools

Publicly accessible and sophisticated tools are available for a price to intruders of various skill levels. Known as exploit tools, they can be used to determine vulnerabilities and gain entry into targeted systems.

In May 2009, the U.S. Department of Transportation's inspector general issued a warning about vulnerabilities in the U.S. Air Traffic Control ATC system: "Attackers can take advantage of software vulnerabilities in commercial IP products to exploit ATC systems, which is especially worrisome at a time when the Nation is facing increased threats from sophisticated nation-state-sponsored cyber attacks."[9]

Logic Bombs

Logic bombs are a form of sabotage in which a programmer inserts code that causes the program to perform a destructive action when some triggering event occurs, such as termination of the programmer's employment.

Yung-Hsun Lin, a former systems administrator for Medco Health Solutions, was indicted by a federal grand jury on fraud charges for installing a logic bomb on company computers. The logic bomb had the potential to erase prescription information for 60 million Americans, including the creation of dangerous drug combinations in an individual's prescriptions.[10]

Misauthentication

Misauthentication attacks are those that undermine the authentication mechanisms present or in some cases not present in a network. An attacker somehow is able to convince the network security measures they are an entity that should be allowed access to the system. There are many technologies that can be employed to prevent or deter these kinds of attacks by strengthening authentication methods.

Tom Donahue, the top cybersecurity analyst at the Central Intelligence Agency (CIA), told an audience at a power and utility industry trade conference in New Orleans that "cyber attackers have hacked into the computer systems of utility companies outside the U.S. and made demands, in at least one case causing a power outage that affected multiple cities."

The CIA does not know the identities of the attackers, but all attacks were conducted through the internet.

Ralph Logan, principal of the Logan Group, a cybersecurity firm, commented, "Often there are authentication methods that are less than secure. Sometimes there are no authentication methods."[11]

Phishing

Phishing is the process of sending fraudulent emails that may appear legitimate, but that try to get recipients to divulge sensitive personal information that can then be used for illegitimate purposes.

According to the Federal Bureau of Investigation (FBI) website, part of its 2004 Operation Websnare (a coordinated takedown of suspects in more than 160 cybercrime cases with 150,000 victims who lost more than $215 million) involved a phishing incident: "A man in Iowa allegedly sent emails to customers of the MSN ISP from a 'spoofed' MSN email address telling them to update their financial account records with MSN by 'just clicking on this link.' When they did, the information was snapped up ... and not by MSN. The case led us to an internet service provider in India, a 'redirect' service in Austria (a tactic that hides email senders' true identity), and ultimately back to the subject's computer."[12]

Repudiation

Activities on a system are typically monitored, allowing all actions to be traced if later required for audits. If a system's security has been breached, actions can be taken for which there are no records or for which records have been modified, allowing changes to be made or services to be received with no record of them ever taking place. Information modification occurs when unrestricted access to private data is used to modify records. Information integrity cannot be trusted after a system has been compromised.[13]

Repudiation of documents via the use of digital signatures will help with information assurance by preventing unauthorized modification of documents. By digitally certifying that a document has not been altered, "various types of fraud including revenue diversion frauds, procurement frauds and payment frauds" will be prevented.[14]

Sniffer

Synonymous with a packet sniffer, a sniffer is a program that intercepts routed data and examines each packet (unit of formatted data) in search of specified information, such as passwords transmitted in clear text.

In a federal inquiry, three people were charged with illegally accessing and stealing credit card numbers by hacking into cash register terminals, using a packet sniffer, at 11 Dave & Buster's restaurants.[15]

Spam

Spam is unsolicited email. This internet "junk mail" slows down computers and creates extra work (and annoyance) for the email recipient. Many people have lost money to fraudulent spam offers. The U.S. Federal Trade Commission has an information page on spam and the CAN-SPAM law (www.ftc.gov/spam).[16]

According to the FBI, one of its Operation Websnare cases involved spamming. "A Los Angeles-area man allegedly stole thousands of valid email addresses from a previous employer and sold them online. He was also a 'wireless spammer,' driving around LA using unsecured residential wireless networks to broadcast pornography ads from his laptop."[17]

Spoofing

Spoofing involves sending email that appears to originate from one source but was actually sent from a different source. Spoofers often try to trick the recipient into divulging passwords or other sensitive information.

By intercepting and diverting the text messages from the mobile devices of Sandton Hilton hotel guests, hackers obtained login details from the individuals and made transactions from their accounts, using a one-time password.[18]

Spyware

Spyware is a computer program that collects personal information about the user without their consent. It works in numerous ways, including keystroke reading and tracking web-browsing history.

GoldenCashWorld, a one-stop online network for people who buy and sell access to infected computers, was discovered by security researchers in early 2009. Infected PCs were used to send spam, collect personal information, or spread malicious code. Included in this package were tools for creating malicious code and stolen credentials for about 100,000 websites. The network was based in Russia, and about 40 percent of the compromised computers belonged to U.S. individuals or companies.[19]

System Malfunction

System malfunction attacks exploit some accidental deficiency in a system, such as software bugs, misconfigured equipment, or insecure protocols. Much harder to protect against than misauthentication, these attacks prey on unintended operational behavior. The only way to prevent this type of attack is to design, develop, and deploy bug-free network tools, a task that has proved to be a long-standing challenge.

An attacker could also wreak havoc by reconfiguring a system for utter chaos or other devious intentions. A system modification would sufficiently compromise systems by replaying, rerouting, misrouting, or deleting messages, or preventing connection. Imagine the security implications if sensitive communications were retransmitted to a hostile entity.

Taiwan Premier Chang Chun-hsiung announced that the Central Election Commission's (CEC's) website had been attacked by the Chinese cyber army. "We detected some attempts to hack into the CEC's website servers. The hackers attempted to cause our computer server to crash or malfunction in order to hamper election preparations."[20]

Theft of Information

Sensitive, important financial information or private data can be stolen during the course of an attack. This is known as theft of information.

In July 2009, someone hacked into the email account of a Twitter employee. The stolen information included passwords to the employee's Google Apps account. The Google account was accessed, and the hacker retrieved a Twitter financial forecast. The theft of information from the popular social media website is raising valid questions about password protection and the safety of "cloud computing, software and technologies that reside on an Internet server, rather than on individual computers."[21]

Hackers broke into the computer networks of Sonoma State University in California and the University of North Texas and may have accessed 100,000 identities, including Social Security numbers.[22]

Theft of Service

Probably the most common type of attack in telephony, theft of service involves the use of resources for which there is no compensation (e.g., free long-distance services). Voice over Internet Protocol (VoIP) PBX systems are a cost-saving and flexible IP-based alternative to traditional circuit-switched phone systems. As with traditional systems,

VoIP PBX systems have risks including DoS attacks, privacy breaches, and theft of services.

"Securing a VoIP PBX presents some unique challenges, but the alternative—loss of service and, possibly, loss of customers—may be more costly in the long run."[23]

Tracking

Government agencies and law enforcement can track people through signals emanating from cellular technology. Suspects can be monitored, which raises privacy issues.

"Police in Los Angeles have tested a device that shoots a 'sticky' GPS locator onto the rear of a fleeing car, letting the cops pull back from dangerous car chases and track a perp's movements via cellular technology. The unit, called the StarChase Tagging and Tracking Pursuit Management System or SCTTPMS for, er, short, uses a laser-sighted, compressed air cannon mounted on the front of a police cruiser to shoot a miniature GPS receiver embedded in an epoxy compound. … 'It has real James Bond appeal,' says Sergeant Dan Gomez with the LAPD's Tactical Technology Unit."[24]

According to Wired.com, the LAPD planned to have this equipment available by early 2007, but by 2011 the police department had yet to implement it.[25]

Trojan Horse

Computer programs can contain harmful code. A Trojan horse usually masquerades as a useful program that a user wants to execute.

A Trojan horse program was found on a computer in a drug-testing lab in Châtenay-Malabry, France, that allowed outsiders to remotely download files related to American cyclist Floyd Landis.[26]

Unauthorized Access

An attacker can gain access to billing information, personal information, or other information that is not meant for public disclosure.

According to the FBI, part of its Operation Websnare involved "a Romanian computer hacker and his five American accomplices who were indicted for allegedly conspiring to steal more than $10 million in computer equipment from a California computer equipment supplier after hacking into its computer system."[27]

Carleton University charged a student with unauthorized use of a computer after he hacked into 32 electronic accounts, using a program that recorded keystrokes.[28]

Unauthorized Use of Resources

Unauthorized use of resources involves acting on data to which an attacker is not entitled, including bandwidth.

One example demonstrates the serious nature of such use. An inspector general's report issued in March 2008 indicated that the Department of Defense oversight of security procedures used by BAE Systems to ensure that classified technology and information not be accessed by unauthorized parties posed "the risk of unintended or deliberate release of information to foreign competitors" in the F-35 Jet program.[29]

Viruses

A virus is a program that "infects" computer files, usually an executable program, by inserting a copy of itself into the file. These copies are usually executed when the infected file is loaded into memory, allowing the virus to infect other files. Unlike a computer worm, a virus usually requires unwitting human involvement.

David L. Smith, of Monmouth County, New Jersey, pleaded guilty and was convicted of emailing the "Melissa" virus from his home computer and disrupting computers worldwide in 1999. Smith was sentenced to 20 months in federal prison and was fined $5,000. The virus caused more than $80 million in damages.[30]

On May 17, 2009, a computer virus was discovered that forced the emergency dispatch system in Dallas, Texas, to be shut down for several hours.[31]

Vishing

Vishing is a method of phishing based on VoIP technology and open source call center software. Scammers set up phony call centers, and then send emails or text messages notifying potential victims that there has been a security problem. Potential victims are instructed to call their banks to reactivate a credit or debit card, or to contact a fake online bank to renew their accounts.

War-Driving

War-driving is a method of gaining entry into wireless computer networks using a laptop, antennas, and a wireless network adaptor, and involves patrolling locations to gain unauthorized access. War-driving is an updated version of the crime war-dialing, portrayed in the 1983 movie *War Games*, in which a simple computer program dials consecutive phone numbers looking for modems.

Eleven international suspects, including a U.S. Secret Service informant, were charged with fraud using war-driving software to extract customer credit card information from stores including T.J.Maxx and Barnes & Noble.[32]

Worms

Worms are independent computer programs that reproduce by copying themselves from one system to another across a network. Unlike computer viruses, worms do not require human involvement to propagate.

In November 1988, the Morris worm brought 10 percent of internet systems to a halt.

See the Introduction and Chapter 5 for more information on the infamous Stuxnet worm.

Zero-Day Exploit

A zero-day exploit is a cyberthreat that takes advantage of a security vulnerability on the same day that the vulnerability becomes known to the general public. There are no available fixes.

Who Carries Out Attacks?

Bot-Network Operators

Bot-network operators use a network, or botnet, of compromised, remotely controlled systems to coordinate attacks and to distribute phishing schemes, spam, and malware attacks. The services of these networks are sometimes made available on underground markets.

Criminal Groups

International corporate spies and organized crime organizations pose a threat to the U.S. through their ability to conduct industrial espionage and large-scale monetary theft, and to hire or develop hacker talent.

In 2008, cyber criminals in the U.K. made "a festive fortune by flogging stolen Facebook profiles for just 89 [pence] each."[33]

"Cyber criminals are one of the fastest growing security threats. Other factors that increase online criminal activity include the popularity of social networking and other online communications, online banking and finance, organized crime, and the current economic recession."[34]

Cyberterrorists

Cyberterrorists have gained a great deal of international attention recently. This group attacks with the intent of creating the most high-profile, prominent, and chaotic incidents possible. Al-Qaida is believed to be among the ranks of cyberterrorists.

The Department of Homeland Security released a video with disturbing images from a demonstration by the Idaho National Laboratory on March 4, 2007. During a computer simulation of a hacker attack against the U.S. electrical grid, smoke began pouring from an expensive electrical turbine. "It's so graphic," said Amit Yoran, U.S. cybersecurity chief during the George W. Bush administration. "Talking about bits and bytes doesn't have the same impact as seeing something catch fire."[35]

The Honorable Yvette D. Clarke, chairwoman of the Committee on Homeland Security in the U.S. House of Representatives, released this statement during negotiations of the security of the modern electric grid: "Cyber and physical attacks against the grid could both be catastrophic and incredibly destructive events, but they are not inevitable. Protections can—and must—be put in place ahead of time to mitigate the impact of these attacks.[36]

Disgruntled Employees

Current or former employees with a grudge often represent the most difficult type of attacker to defend against. The disgruntled organization insider is a principal source of computer crimes. Insiders may not need a great deal of knowledge about computer intrusions because their knowledge of a victim system often allows them to gain unrestricted access to damage the system or to steal system data. The insider threat also includes outsourcing vendors. This group leaves Trusted Networks (TNs) at a huge disadvantage due to its specialized knowledge of the intricate details of TN operations and vulnerabilities.

In early 2009, Deloitte Global Financial Services released a report stating that disgruntled employees are one of the major risks to IT systems. Kris Budnik, director of enterprise risk services at Deloitte, said, "On one front is the growing sophistication of attacks and the magnitude and frequency of data losses and breaches of customer information. On the other front are the growing regulatory expectations in a challenging economic environment and the massive layoffs that result in a distracted or insecure workforce and disgruntled employees."[37]

Hackers or Hacktivists

Hackers sometimes crack into networks for the thrill of the challenge or for bragging rights in the hacker community. While remote cracking once required a fair amount of skill or computer knowledge, hackers can now download attack scripts from the internet and launch them against victim sites. So, while attack tools have become more sophisticated, they have also become easier to use. According to the CIA, the large majority of hackers do not have the requisite tradecraft to threaten difficult targets such as critical U.S. networks. Nevertheless, the worldwide population of hackers poses a relatively high threat of an isolated or brief disruption causing serious damage.

Whether attacking for reasons ranging from recreation to social/political motivation, this group represents an assortment of skills and intent. Hackers quite likely represent the most common type of attacker a TN will face.

"Hacktivism" refers to politically motivated attacks on publicly accessible webpages or email servers. These groups and individuals overload email servers and hack into websites to send a political message. Most international hacktivist groups appear bent on propaganda rather than damage to critical infrastructures.

Early in 2009, a 10-month investigation by the Information Warfare Monitor uncovered a Chinese electronic spy network that infiltrated 1,295 government office computers in 103 countries. Hackers compromised computers with malware, sending and receiving classified data.[38]

Intruders (Insiders or Physical Intruders)

While external intruders try to gain access to systems from outside of the normal operational setup, this class establishes a physical presence on the inside of the system. In this case, the attacker can operate in what are often less restrictive environments behind a system's external defenses.

The most difficult class of attack comes from the inside. This attack springs from those who are a trusted part of the system's operational activities. Such individuals do not need to defeat many security measures because they have been given authorized access to system resources.

The U.K.'s Financial Services Authority acknowledges that not all financial institutions understand that data is a valuable commodity for criminals. This causes them to overlook vulnerable areas such as malicious insider activity. The U.K.'s fraud prevention service, the Credit Industry Fraud Avoidance System, "believes that fraudsters often solicit the help of existing employees in their attempt to procure valuable data." Urs Fischer, vice president and head of information technology governance and risk management at pension and life insurer Swiss Life, says the internal threat is his No. 1 concern. "For me, the danger is coming from the inside ... The tactics deployed in such instances might include social engineering, a tried and tested method in which fraudsters effectively 'trick' employees into revealing information, or though financial inducement. ... Incompetence is one thing, but you can build awareness. I think [the threat] is more malicious."[39]

In its recent Crimewatch survey conducted for the U.S. Secret Service, Carnegie Mellon University's Computer Emergency Response Team found that "two-thirds of insider-enabled data theft involved an external colluder to whom the information was sold. ... In half of these cases the individual was actively recruited for the task."[40]

Nations or States

Several nations are aggressively working to develop information warfare doctrine, programs, and capabilities. Such capabilities enable a single entity to have a significant and serious impact by disrupting the supply, communications, and economic infrastructures that support military power—impacts that could affect the daily lives of U.S. citizens across the country. The threat from national cyber warfare programs is unique because the threat extends along the entire spectrum of objectives that might harm U.S. interests. According to the CIA, only government-sponsored programs are developing capabilities with the prospect of causing widespread, long-duration damage to critical U.S. infrastructures.

The newly created U.S. Cybercommand, and similar Chinese, North Korean, and Russian initiatives, are the most visible forces. Estonia is training the North Atlantic Treaty Organization's future cyberwarriors, and the European Union is expressing concern over the subject. Germany claims the Chinese government is behind attacks on German companies and government organizations. Palestinians and Israelis have engaged in cyberwar for several years, and Iran claims to be in a cyberwar with the Israel Defense Forces. India created a regional cybersecurity and research center.

As the superiority of the U.S. military services continues to grow, enemy states will undoubtedly seek other methods for attacking our nation. Cyberwarfare is undoubtedly an attractive tool to serve as amplification for limited resources and an alternative to conventional warfare. Some of these attackers are believed to be pro-American.

Russia's attacks on Estonia and Georgia are prime examples of one hostile nation attacking another nation's cyberspace.

Early in 2010, Google experienced "highly sophisticated" attacks as well as theft of intellectual property that originated in China. In protest, Google announced in January 2010 that it would no longer perform the required Chinese government censoring of Google search engine results. In addition, the U.S. government lodged a formal protest against China.[41]

Several months later, Google disclosed that some of the passwords of its millions of users were included in the intellectual property stolen in January 2010. Chinese hackers had access to Google internet services, including email and business applications.[42]

Phishers

Individuals or small groups execute phishing schemes in an attempt to steal identities or information for monetary gain. Phishers may also use spam and spyware or malware to accomplish their objectives.

Spammers

Individuals and organizations distribute unsolicited email with hidden or false information in order to sell products, conduct phishing schemes, distribute spyware or malware, or attack organizations (i.e., DoS).

Spyware and Malware Authors

Spyware and malware authors are posing an increasingly serious threat. Individuals and organizations with malicious intent carry out attacks against users by producing and distributing spyware and malware. Several destructive computer viruses and worms have harmed files and hard drives, including the Melissa Macro Virus, the Explore.Zip worm, the CIH (Chernobyl) Virus, Nimda, Code Red, Slammer, and Blaster.

A paradigm shift to emerging markets is occurring with spyware and malware authors and their intended victims. Mikko Hypponen, chief research officer of F-Secure in Helsinki, Finland, discussed a recent F-Secure report that shows a trend in new ecriminal groups originating in countries that are adapting to sophisticated technology. "Brazil today has over two million internet users and coincidentally, since 2003 computer crime has taken off in Brazil as well as China and former Soviet countries."[43]

Terrorists

Terrorists seek to destroy, incapacitate, or exploit critical infrastructures to threaten national security, to cause mass casualties, to weaken the U.S. economy, and to damage public morale and confidence. However, traditional terrorist adversaries of the U.S. are less developed in their computer network capabilities than other adversaries. Terrorists are likely to pose a limited cyberthreat. The CIA believes terrorists will stay focused on traditional attack methods, but it anticipates increased cyberthreats as a more technically competent generation enters the ranks.

Sri Lanka's Liberation Tigers of Tamil Eelam terrorist group won a round of cyberwarfare, crippling the country's infrastructure for a few days. Hamas has declared cyberwar on Israel. The U.K. remains concerned about Al-Qaida plans for cyberwar against Britain.

Trusted Clients

A "trusted client" has access that is not available to the public via its close affiliation with the service provider being targeted for an attack.

Contractor and subcontractors have often been responsible for information theft. In 2007, the FBI investigated the prime contractor Unisys Corporation "after it allegedly failed to detect cyber break-ins traced to a Chinese-language website and then tried to cover up its deficiencies." Unisys Corporation is a major information technology firm, winning two Department of Homeland Security contracts in 2002 and 2005 that were worth $1.7 billion. [44]

Endnotes

1. Cynthia Karena, "A New Security Frontier: It's All About the Data," *The Age*, June 3, 2008, 7.

2. Evan T. Grim and Michael W. Raschke, "National Communications System Technical Information Bulletin 05-4: Cyber Vulnerabilities within Telecommunication Supervisory Control and Data Acquisition Systems," National Communications System, May 2005, accessed July 18, 2011, www.ncs.gov/library/tech_bulletins/2005/tib_05-4.pdf, 14.

3. Ian Fette, "How To Avoid Getting Hooked," Google Blog, April 29, 2008, accessed June 8, 2011, googleblog.blogspot.com/2008/04/how-to-avoid-getting-hooked. html.

4. Grim, "National Communications System Technical Information Bulletin," 14.

5. Jessica E. Vascellaro, and Ben Worthen, "Twitter, Facebook Sites Disrupted by Web Attack," *Wall Street Journal*, August 6, 2009, A2.

6. Stephen Mihm, "Acoustic Keyboard Eavesdropping," *New York Times Magazine*, December 12, 2004, 50.

7. "Report of the Commission to Assess the Threat to the United States from Electromagnetic Pulse EMP Attack," EMP Commission, April 2008, accessed June 8, 2011, www.empcommission.org/docs/A2473-EMP_Commission-7MB.pdf.

8. James Risen, "F.B.I. Seizes Computer Drive in a China Nuclear Inquiry," *New York Times*, July 20, 2000, 19.

9. Federal Aviation Administration, "Review of Web Applications Security and Intrusion Detection in Air Traffic Control Systems, FI-2009-049," U.S. Department of Transportation, May 4, 2009, accessed June 8, 2011, www.oig.dot.gov/sites/dot/files/pdfdocs/ATC_Web_Report.pdf.

10. Ronald Smothers, "U.S. Says Ex-Worker at Drug Giant Was Out to Damage Computer Data," *New York Times*, December 20, 2006, B1.

11. Ellen Nakashima and Steven Mufson, "Hackers Have Attacked Foreign Utilities, CIA Analyst Says," *Washington Post,* January 19, 2008, A4.

12. "OPERATION 'WEB SNARE': Tightening the Net on Cyber Criminals," U.S. Federal Bureau of Investigation, August 27, 2004, accessed June 8, 2011, www2.fbi.gov/page2/aug04/websnare082704.htm.

13. Grim, "National Communications System Technical Information Bulletin," 14.

14. Tim Best, "The Rise of Fraud," *Computer Weekly,* January 29, 2008, accessed June 8, 2011, www.computerweekly.com/Articles/2008/01/21/228999/The-rise-of-fraud.htm.

15. "Hackers Indicted for Stealing Credit and Debit Card Numbers From National Restaurant Chain," U.S. Department of Justice, May 12, 2008, accessed June 8, 2011, www.justice.gov/criminal/cybercrime/yastremskiyIndict.pdf.

16. "Spam: Introduction," Federal Trade Commission, accessed June 8, 2011, www.ftc.gov/spam.

17. "OPERATION 'WEB SNARE.'"

18. "Phish, Spoof and Woof! It's Gone," *Sunday Times (South Africa),* July 19, 2009, CRIME, LAW & JUSTICE section.

19. Deborah Gage, "Ring Sells Access to Computers," *San Francisco Chronicle,* June 17, 2009, C1.

20. "Taiwan Premier Says China Tried to Hack Taiwan Election Board Network," *BBC Monitoring International Reports,* January 5, 2008.

21. John D. Sutter, "Twitter Hack Raises Questions About Cloud Computing," CNN, July 16, 2009, accessed June 8, 2011, www.cnn.com/2009/TECH/07/16/twitter.hack/index.html.

22. Martin J. Garvey, "Web Services' Security Factor—Basic Practices Such as Authentication Can Protect Web Services From Hackers and Limit Access to Authorized Personnel," *Information Week,* August 8, 2005, 55.

23. Peter Morrissey, "Safe Sound-And Data: Safeguarding an IP PBX Presents Some Challenges, But Basic Measures Can Help," *Information Week,* December 1, 2008, 39.

24. Neil Vorano, "Police Tech Goes James Bond-ish," *National Post,* October 12, 2007, DT16.

25. Wired Blogs, "Tag You're a Criminal," Wired.com, May 10, 2006, accessed June 8, 2011, www.wired.com/autopia/2006/05/tag_youre_a_cri.

26. David Jolly, "Cycling Inquiry Exposes Corporate World of Spies and Hackers," *International Herald Tribune,* August 1, 2009, 11.

27. "OPERATION 'WEB SNARE.'"

28. "Carleton Student Charged With Hacking," *National Post Canada,* September 12, 2008, A6.

29. Dana Hedgpeth, "Security of F-35 Jet Secrets Questioned; 'Incomplete' Oversight May Have Allowed Leaks, Report Says," *Washington Post,* May 2, 2008, D1.

30. Jeremy Pearce, "Melissa Virus," *New York Times,* May 5, 2002, 6.

31. Tanya Eiserer, "Dallas' Emergency Dispatch Computers Are Latest Virus Victim," *Dallas Morning News,* May 19, 2009, 3B.

32. Ibid.

33. Jonathan Weinberg, "Facecrooks: Hackers Sell Networking Details to Gangs," *The Sun (U.K.),* December 16, 2008, 26.

34. Center for Security & Privacy Solutions, "Cyber Crime: A Clear and Present Danger," Deloitte, January 2010, accessed June 8, 2011, www.deloitte.com/view/en_US/us/Insights/centers/Center-Security-and-Privacy-Solutions/bcdc005f1e056210VgnVCM100000ba42f00aRCRD.htm.

35. "U.S. Video Shows Hacker Hit on Power Grid," *USA Today,* September 27, 2007, accessed June 8, 2011, www.usatoday.com/tech/news/computersecurity/2007-09-27-hacker-video_N.htm.

36. Yvette Clarke, "Modern Electric Grid Security." FDCH Congressional Testimony, July 21, 2009, accessed July 18, 2011, www.gpo.gov/fdsys/pkg/CHRG-111hhrg53425/html/CHRG-111hhrg534 25.htm.

37. Sanchia Temkin, "Disgruntled Employees a 'Risk' to Company IT Systems," *Business Day (South Africa)*, February 05, 2009, LABOUR section.

38. "Around the World," *Washington Post*, March 29, 2009, A11.

39. Michelle Price, "Plugging The Leak: The Banking Industry Has Suffered A Number Of Huge Data Breaches," *The Banker,* August 1, 2008, TECHNOLOGY section.

40. Ibid.

41. Bruce Einhorn, Tom Giles, and Douglas MacMillan, "Google And China: A Win For Liberty—And Strategy," *Businessweek,* January 25, 2010, 35.

42. John Markoff, "Cyberattack on Google Said to Hit Password System," *New York Times,* April 20, 2010, A1.

43. Hazimin Sulaiman, "Shift to Emerging Markets," *New Straits Times (Malaysia),* January 28, 2008, accessed June 8, 2011, findarticles.com/p/news-articles/new-straits-times/mi_8016/is_20080128/shift-emerging-markets/ai_n44388635.

44. Ellen Nakashima and Brian Krebs, "Contractor Blamed in DHS Data Breaches," *Washington Post*, September 24, 2007, accessed June 8, 2011, www.washingtonpost.com/wp-dyn/content/article/2007/09/23/AR2007092301471.html.

About the Contributors

Amber Benham is a Brooklyn-based multimedia journalist specializing in all things edible. Her love for storytelling across media platforms took her to *Saveur* magazine and *Edible Manhattan*, where she helped the magazine grow its online presence and include more multimedia food stories. She currently freelances as a reporter for several New York publications. When she isn't crime reporting for the *Wall Street Journal* or researching traditional Ukrainian wedding bread, she teaches middle school students how to read and write. She earned a master's degree in interactive journalism from the CUNY Graduate School of Journalism.

Eli Edwards is a web consultant and information professional with academic and special library experience, including legal research. He is also an attorney in good standing in the State of California. His research interests fall under the umbrella of information policy, including internet speech, online privacy, media law and regulation, government transparency, and the ethics of information retrieval in a Web 2.0 world. In addition to an MLIS from San Jose State University, Edwards also holds a JD from Santa Clara University School of Law.

Ben Fractenberg is a reporter and multimedia producer for the news site DNAinfo. His work has appeared in publications including the *New York Times*, Fort Greene-Clinton Hill blog, Haaretz, *Daily News*, DNAinfo, and the *Huffington Post*. He has also worked with various nonprofits, including Public Allies, where he helped develop young leaders for a career in public service, and the Gay and Lesbian Alliance Against Defamation, where he ensured fair representations of the LGBT community in the media. Fractenberg earned a master's degree from the CUNY Graduate School of Journalism, where he won a small grant to create an internet startup that connects editors with citizen journalists. The site, called Local Desk, went live in summer 2010.

Laura Gordon-Murnane has worked as the intranet webmaster for a legal publisher located near Washington, D.C., for more than 12 years. Gordon-Murnane is frequently published in *Searcher Magazine*, *ONLINE*, and Information Today, Inc.'s *NewsBreaks*. She has delivered professional presentations at the Special Libraries Association's annual conference and at WebSearch University's annual conference in Washington, D.C. In 2005, *Library Journal* named her a Mover and Shaker. She earned an MLS from the University of Maryland and an MA and BA in history from Indiana University, Bloomington.

Cynthia Hetherington, MLS, MSM, is the founder of Hetherington Group, a firm dedicated to private, corporate, and government investigation and security using the industry's most highly regarded and nationally known investigative experts. The group provides corporate security officials; military intelligence units; and federal, state, and local law enforcement agencies with training in online intelligence practices, techniques, and insights. A widely published author, Hetherington has written *Business Background Investigations* and *The Manual to Online Public Records*. She publishes the Data2know.com: Internet & Online Intelligence Newsletter and has co-authored articles on steganography, computer forensics, internet investigations, and security-focused monographs.

Deborah A. Liptak, MLIS, is the president of info2go, a company that provides consulting and training to small and medium-sized businesses that need answers to strategic questions. The company also specializes in locating, analyzing, and delivering solutions beyond what is available on the free internet. info2go's areas of expertise include competitive intelligence, industry information, market research, and research instruction. Liptak is also a part-time counselor and instructor with Tarrant County College Small Business Development Center, where she facilitates FastTrac classes and teaches distance learning market research classes. She earned an MLIS degree from the University of Oklahoma in 1988 and has 5 years of experience as a communications-electronics officer in the U.S. Air Force.

Anne P. Mintz spent several decades as the director of information centers in media and investment banking before becoming a freelance business researcher, writer, and editor. Her current endeavors include working on behalf of publishers to present their content online in searchable formats. She is the editor of *Web of Deception: Misinformation on the Internet* (CyberAge Books, 2002) and a variety of articles about databases and the quality of information retrieved online. Mintz has taught at the graduate-school level in journalism and information science. She holds a BA in English from the University of Massachusetts and an MLS from Rutgers University.

Meg Smith spent a decade at the *Washington Post* as a news researcher. She was the lead researcher for the paper's coverage of the shootings at Virginia Tech, which won the Pulitzer Prize for Breaking News Reporting in 2008 and was a landmark for how the newspaper used social networking sites to report the news. She researched Gene Weingarten's feature story "Fatal Distraction," which won the Pulitzer Prize for Feature Writing in 2010. Smith has spoken at numerous conferences in recent years about how researchers can verify and use social media to enhance journalism and law enforcement investigations. She has a bachelor's degree in journalism and an MLS, both from the University of Maryland.

Craig Thompson is an experienced journalist, researcher, and TV producer. He recently completed work on a research project with the Center for International Media Assistance, investigating worldwide licensing procedures for journalists. He works as a researcher for the American Theater Wing and as a reporter and researcher for MSN and Reuters. He also produces broadcast segments at CUNY TV. In the past, he has held positions at Nielsen Business Media and ESPN Books. He has experience as a professional blogger covering emerging technologies such as the iPad and virtual worlds. He also earned a graduate degree from the CUNY Graduate School of Journalism.

INDEX

A

accountability news, 116–117

accountability organizations, 127–128

accounts, closing online, 38

Accuracy in Media, 124

Accurint (public records business), 26

Acxiom (public records business), 26–27

Adair, Bill, 118

ADL (Anti-Defamation League), 46

"Adnali for Turkstorm.Org," 90

ad serving, 139, 140

advance fee fraud, 74

Ahmadinejad, Mahmoud, 14

AirKatrina.com, 136

Ambinder, Marc, 118–119

Anderson, Tom, 10

Angle, Sharron, 49

Angwin, Julie, 10

"Anonymous" hacktivist group, 89, 90

Anti-Defamation League (ADL), 46

apartment rental scams, 60–61

applications, techniques to keep personal information offline, 30

Armistead, Leigh, 83

Arrington, Michael, 8

art forgeries, spotting, 2

associational distortion, 47, 54

asymmetrical warfare. *See* information warfare

ATM cards, reporting fraud, 75

auction fraud, 65–66, 75

Awad, Muneer, 49–50

B

Baby Manuela hoax, 137

backfire effect of facts, 115

background checks, 25

banks, techniques to keep personal information offline, 30

Belarus, information warfare involving, 90

Better Business Bureau (BBB), 76, 77, 141–142, 146

Bevan, Tom, 126

bias in media, evaluating, 124–125

"birther" rumor, 108–109, 121

Black, Derek, 44

Black, Don, 44

blackmail scams, Facebook, 7–8

blogs, 30, 45, 120, 126–127. *See also* Twitter

Border Patrol (online game), 41, 52

Bosnian conflict, information warfare during, 85–86

botnets, 87–88

Brandeis, Louis D., 50

Breer, Paul, 124

Buck, James, 14

Burma, communications restrictions by, 94

business, preparedness for information warfare, 97

C

cable television, during crises, 93
CAO (Ireland's Central
    Applications Office), infor-
    mation warfare attack on, 88
cashier's checks, fraudulent, 64, 65,
    76
Center for Media and Democracy,
    124
Center for Neighborhood
    Technology, 101–102
Center for Public Integrity, 136
Center for Responsive Politics, 127
Central Applications Office (CAO),
    information warfare attack
    on, 88
challenge questions, 37
charitable organizations, tax forms
    for, 141–142, 143–144, 146
CharityChoices.com, 142–143
Charity Commission, U.K., 134
Charity Navigator website, 135,
    140–141, 144, 145
"Charity Rating Guide & Watchdog
    Report" (Charity Watch), 143
charity scams
    avoiding, 134–136, 138,
        139–140, 144–147
    disaster relief, 133–134,
        135–137, 145
    reporting, 146
    search engine ad serving, 139
    United Kingdom, 133–134
    watchdog organizations,
        134–135, 137, 140–143
Charity Watch, 143
checks, background, 25
checks, fraudulent, 76. *See also*
    cashier's checks, fraudulent

children, on Facebook, 31–32, 33,
    34–35
China, information warfare involv-
    ing, 91
Church of Scientology, information
    warfare against, 90
citizen journalism, 120
climate change issue, 111–113,
    118–119
CNN, distributed denial of service
    attacks against, 91
cognitive dissonance, 113–114, 116
communications security, defined,
    99
communications systems, 100–101
communications zone, 82
computer crimes, 74
Computer Security Report Card, 97
confirmation bias, 114
conflict, avoidance of psychologi-
    cal, 113–114, 116
conflict and strategy frame,
    111–112
Congress, public view of U.S.,
    110–111
contact information on websites, 71
Cooper, Abraham, 46
craigslist, 16, 60–61, 64
Crawford, George A., 84, 96
credit cards
    fraud, 58, 75
    keeping personal information
        offline, 26, 30
    legislation affecting, 25
    monitoring accuracy, 26
    safety of purchasing with, 58,
        75, 77
credit reports, 25, 26, 29
Crist, Charlie, 136
crowdsourcing, described, 14

More CyberAge Books from Information Today, Inc.

Web of Deception
Misinformation on the Internet

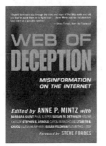

Edited by Anne P. Mintz
Foreword by Steve Forbes

Intentionally misleading or erroneous information on the web can wreak havoc on your health, privacy, investments, business decisions, online purchases, legal affairs, and more. Until now, the breadth and significance of this growing problem for internet users have yet to be fully explored. In *Web of Deception*, Anne P. Mintz brings together 10 information industry gurus to illuminate the issues and help you recognize and deal with the flood of deception and misinformation in a range of critical subject areas. A must-read for any internet searcher who needs to evaluate online information sources and avoid web traps.

278 pp/softbound/ISBN 0-910965-60-9 $24.95

The Extreme Searcher's Internet Handbook, 3rd Edition
A Guide for the Serious Searcher

By Randolph Hock

The Extreme Searcher's Internet Handbook is the essential guide for anyone who uses the internet for research—librarians, teachers, students, writers, business professionals, and others who need to search the web proficiently. In this fully updated third edition, Ran Hock covers strategies and tools for all major areas of internet content. Readers with little to moderate searching experience will appreciate Hock's helpful, easy-to-follow advice, while experienced searchers will discover a wealth of new ideas, techniques, and resources.

368 pp/softbound/ISBN 978-0-910965-84-2 $24.95

Research on Main Street
Using the Web to Find Local Business and Market Information

By Marcy Phelps

Even in a global economy, businesses need targeted, localized information about customers, companies, and industries. But as skilled searchers know, adding the element of geography to any research project creates new challenges. With *Research on Main Street*, Marcy Phelps presents a unique and useful guide to finding business and market information about places—including counties, cities, census blocks, and other sub-state areas—using free and low-cost online resources. You'll learn expert techniques and strategies for approaching location-specific research, including advice on how to tap local sources for in-depth information about business and economic conditions, issues, and outlooks. In addition to sharing her own well-honed expertise, Phelps incorporates a wealth of advice from her fellow business researchers throughout. Don't miss the author's companion website at www.ResearchOnMainStreet.com!

280 pp/softbound/ISBN 978-0-910965-88-0 $29.95

Dancing With Digital Natives
Staying in Step With the Generation That's Transforming the Way Business Is Done

Edited by Michelle Manafy and Heidi Gautschi

Generational differences have always influenced how business is done, but in the case of digital natives—those immersed in digital technology from birth—we are witnessing a tectonic shift. As an always connected, socially networked generation increasingly dominates business and society, organizations can ignore the implications only at the risk of irrelevance. In this fascinating book, Michelle Manafy, Heidi Gautschi, and a stellar assemblage of experts from business and academia provide vital insights into the characteristics of this transformative generation. Here is an in-depth look at how digital natives work, shop, play, and learn, along with practical advice geared to help managers, marketers, coworkers, and educators maximize their interactions and create environments where everyone wins.

408 pp/hardbound/ISBN 978-0-910965-87-3 $27.95

31901051422790